DEPRESSION TIMES COOKBOOK

by

Bruce Carlson

© *1993 by Bruce Carlson*

All rights reserved. No part of this book may be reproduced or transmitted in any form or by any means, electronic or mechanical, including photocopying, recording or by any informational storage or retrieval system, except by a reviewer who may quote brief passages in a review to be printed in a magazine or newspaper-without permission in writing from the publisher.

* * * * * * * * *

**QUIXOTE PRESS
3544 Blakslee St.
Wever, IA 52658
1-800-571-2665**

PRINTED
IN
U.S.A.

DEDICATION

-to all those folks who recall a soup gettin' stretched with water to cover one more mouth, and a salad bein' made larger with greens from the woods.

TABLE OF CONTENTS

Appetizers and Beverages 13-30

Salads 31-48

Soups 49-56

Main Dishes 57-94

Breads 95-104

Cakes 'N Muffins 'N Such 105-116

Desserts 117-156

Bars and Cookies 157-188

Candy 189-198

Miscellaneous 199-210

ACKNOWLEDGEMENTS

Thanks a lot, Ella, Susan, Hilma, Ery, and Clarindia for your help in pulling together these recipes from "way back then".

PREFACE

It all started out with my thinking that a book on Depression cooking was one that had a bunch of cheap ingredients in it.

Well, I did my research and found it was more than that. The Depression was a slice of history, too. And, this cookbook leads us to many of the mouth-watering recipes of the American Midwest in the early 1930's.

x

INTRODUCTION

My friends who have enough years behind them tell me that the smells and tastes of many of these recipes seem to roll back the years. They roll back the years to when they remember coming home from school and having their mothers greet them with a smile and some of these goodies.

- Prof Phil Hey
Briar Cliff College
Sioux City, Iowa

xii

APPETIZERS and BEVERAGES

APPETIZERS AND BEVERAGES

All Gone Cinnamon Cider 16
Apple-Cherry Drink...15
Aunt Ida's Fruit Dip 23
Betty's Caramel Puff Corn..26
Bloody Marys 19
Broiled Walnut Stuffed Mushrooms 16
Carameled Popcorn 29
Cheese Ball 26
Cheese Bread Sticks 29
Crawdaddy Dip...25
Crockpot Cider Makin's 20
Curried Chicken Logs 27
Deviled Eggs 27
Dill Dip 24
Drink Made with Juices...22
Evening Snack Dip..22
Frosted River Bottom Walnuts 19
Hog Heaven Ham Balls 30
Hot Cider Punch 17
Hot Dried Beef Dip 21
Iced Mocha 18
Kid Stopper Crawdaddy Bites 28
More Drinks Made with Juices.....................................16
Orange Julius 15
Pecan Goodies...23
River Crab Spread 21
Spinach Balls 30
Stawberry Daiquiri 17
Stuffed Timber Mushrooms..25
Tear Fixer Ice Tea Fizz 18
Vegetable Dip..24
Venison Dip 20

Apple Cherry Drink

2 pkgs. cherry Kool-Aid
½ C. sugar
1 (6 ozs.) can frozen lemonade

1½ qt. apple juice
2¼ qt. ice water

Mix and serve cold. Makes 1 gallon.

Orange Julius

½ C. water
⅓ C. milk
3 oz. orange juice concentrate

5 ice cubes
2 tsp. sugar
½ tsp. vanilla

Put in mixer and blend until smooth.

All Gone Cinnamon Cider

1 gallon apple cider

1 C. red hots, imperials candy

Heat cider on stove or in 30-cup coffee server. When hot, stir in the candy and it will dissolve quickly. Adds a pretty pink color to the cider and a mild cinnamon flavor.

Broiled Walnut Stuffed Mushrooms

1 lb. medium to large mushrooms
3 T. butter
¾ C. chopped onion
½ C. soft bread crumbs

¼ C. chopped walnuts
¼ tsp. salt
1/16 tsp. pepper
1½ tsp. dry sherry

Preheat broiler. Rinse and pat dry mushrooms. Remove stems; saving both caps and stems. Chop enough stems to make 1 cup. Melt 1 T. butter. Add chopped mushroom stems and onion. Cook and stir until the moisture has evaporated, 3-4 minutes; remove from heat. Stir in bread crumbs, walnuts, salt, pepper and sherry. Put mushroom caps, hollow side down on baking sheet. Melt remaining 2 T. butter. Brush each cap with butter. Broil until barely tender, about 2 minutes. Turn right side up. Spoon onion-mushroom mixture into caps. Drizzle remaining butter over top. Broil until tops are lightly brown, about 2 minutes.

More Drinks Made With Juices

1 C. pineapple grapefruit juice
½ C. buttermilk
½ C. thawed raspberries or
   strawberries

1 T. wheat germ
4 ice cubes

Combine ingredients in blender on high speed until smooth and well blended. Makes 2¼ cups.

Hot Cider Punch

2 C. cranberry juice
8 C. apple cider
¼ C. brown sugar

2 cinnamon
¾ T. whole cloves
¼ tsp. salt

Place juice and cider in electric percolator. Place all other ingredients in basket. Perk till it shuts off. For a 30 cup pot, use 1 gallon cider, 1 quart cranberry juice and triple spices.

Strawberry Daiquiri

2 (10 oz. ea.) pkgs. frozen strawberries in syrup, partially thawed
½ C. light rum

⅓ C. lime juice
¼ C. confectioners' sugar
2 C. ice cubes

In blender, blend all ingredients, except ice. Gradually add ice, blending till smooth. Makes 1 quart.

Tear Fixer Ice Tea Fizz

1 pt.-1 qt. fresh strawberries
½ C. sugar
5 C. boiling water
1 tea bag

1 (12 oz.) can frozen lemonade, thawed
1 qt. chilled club soda

Combine strawberries and sugar; set aside. In large bowl, pour water over tea bags. Steep for 5 minutes. Cool tea to room temperature. Stir in strawberries and lemonade. Chill and stir in club soda just before serving.

Iced Mocha

2 C. milk
¼ C. Hershey chocolate
1 T. instant coffee

Crushed ice
Vanilla ice cream

Combine milk, Hershey chocolate and instant coffee. Shake and pour over crushed ice. Top with scoop of ice cream.

Bloody Marys

½ C. chopped onion
3 heaping tsp. celery seed
8 oz. vodka
¼ tsp. black pepper
6 oz. lemon juice

½ oz. Worcestershire sauce
1 heaping tsp. sugar
1 tsp. salt
20 oz. vodka
3 qt. V-8 tomato juice

Soak onion, celery seed, vodka and black pepper for 12-24 hours and strain. Add lemon juice, Worcestershire sauce, sugar and salt. Add vodka and V-8 tomato juice; stir. Refrigerate and stir with a dill pickle or celery stalk.

Frosted River Bottom Walnuts

1 egg white, beaten slightly
1 T. water
3 C. walnut meats
½ C. sugar

½ tsp. salt
1 tsp. ground cinnamon
½ tsp. ground cloves
½ tsp. ground nutmeg

In a small bowl, beat together egg white and water until stiff. Stir in walnuts; stirring until all surfaces are moistened. Mix together sugar, salt and spices, sprinkle over walnuts; mixing well. Spread walnuts on a lightly greased or foiled lined cookie sheet and bake in preheated oven at 300° for 30 minutes. Stir twice to crisp and dry walnuts evenly. Makes 3 cups.

Vension Dip

1½ lbs. ground vension
½ lb. Velveeta cheese
1 onion, chopped fine
1 can refried beans

1 can cheddar cheese soup
1 sm. can mild green chilies
1 jar mild taco sauce

Brown ground beef and onion together. Drain off fat. Put rest of ingredients with ground beef and onion in crock pot on low heat. Serve with potato chips or nacho cheese chips.

Crockpot Cider Makin's

2 qts. apple cider
1 pt. cranberry juice
½-¾ C. sugar
1 sm. onion, sliced with peeling

2 sticks cinnamon
¼ C. fresh orange juice
1 C. rum (opt.)

Combine ingredients in crock pot. Cover and cook on high for 2 hours. Remove orange slices and cinnamon sticks. Cook on low for 2-4 hours longer. Serve warm from crock pot.

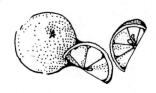

Hot Dried Beef Dip

2 (8 oz. ea.) pkgs. cream cheese
1 (8 oz.) carton sour cream
4 T. milk
4 T. chopped green onions

¼ C. diced green pepper
¼ lb. dried beef, chopped
Parsley, chopped
Nut (opt.)

Beat until smooth the cream cheese, sour cream and milk. Add the remaining ingredients. Bake in a greased casserole and top with parsley and/or nuts; sprinkle with paprika. Bake at 350° for 40 minutes. Serve with Triscuits or cocktail rye bread.

River Crab Spread

13 oz. crab meat
¼ C. tarragon vinegar
⅓ C. mayonnaise or salad dressing
3 T. pimento
2 C. chopped green onion

1 tsp. salt
½ tsp. pepper
1 T. drained capers
Assorted chips, crackers or raw vegetables

Drain crab meat; remove any remaining shell or cartilage. Flake the crab meat. Pour vinegar over crab meat and chill for 30 minutes; drain. Add mayonnaise, pimento, onion, salt and pepper; mix thoroughly. Garnish with capers. Serve with chips, crackers or vegetables.

Drink Made With Juices

1 C. pineapple orange juice
1 (8 oz.) can crushed pineapple with juices
1 egg
1 T. honey
4 ice cubes

Have ingredients chilled. Combine in blender until smooth and well blended on high speed. Makes 2½ cups.

Evening Snack

1 lb. hamburger
1 lb. Velveeta cheese
¼ lb. sharp cheddar cheese
6 oz. jar El Paso hot taco sauce
1 sm. can mushrooms (opt.)

Fry hamburger and onion; drain. Put hamburger, cheeses, hot sauce and mushrooms in crock pot until cheese melts and is well blended. Serve warm with Fritos.

Pecan Goodies

½ C. finely chopped pecans, toasted
1 C. grated cheddar cheese
1½ T. bottled steak sauce
2 T. crumbled crisp bacon

½ C. mayonnaise
2½ dozen crackers or bread rounds

Combine ingredients and spread on crackers. Broil 3 to 4-inches from heat till lightly puffed. Serve hot.

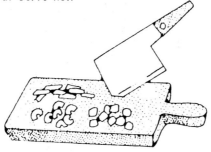

Aunt Ida's Fruit Dip

1 (8 oz.) pkg. cream cheese
½ C. brown sugar

¼ C. powdered sugar
1 tsp. vanilla

Beat all ingredients together with electric mixer. Better, if made day before serving. Especially good with apple slices.

Dill Dip

1 C. sour cream
1 C. mayonnaise
1 T. minced onion
1 tsp. dill weed

1 tsp. Beau Monde spice, Spice
    Island brand
3 tsp. parsley flakes
2 tsp. seasoned salt

Combine all ingredients and chill.

Dill Dip

1 C. sour cream
½ C. Miracle Whip
½ tsp. salt
½ tsp. garlic powder

1 tsp. minced onion
1-2 T. caraway seed
Dash of pepper
Dash of red pepper

Mix all together.

Vegetable Dip

1 C. salad dressing
1 C. sour cream
2 T. minced onions
1 lg. or 2 sm. cloves garlic or salt,
    to taste

1 tsp. salt
½ tsp. pepper
¼ C. parsley (opt.)
1 T. prepared mustard

Combine and refrigerate for 2-3 hours. Serve as dip for carrots, celery sticks, cauliflower, broccoli flowerets, green pepper strips, zucchini wedges and cucumbers.

Stuffed Timber Mushrooms

20-24 mushrooms
Italian dressing
¾ C. soft bread crumbs
6½ oz. can crab meat
2 eggs, beaten

¼ C. chopped onions
½ C. salad dressing or mayonnaise
1 tsp. lemon juice
Cheddar cheese

Remove stems from mushrooms. Sprinkle mushroom cap with Italian dressing; set aside. Combine bread crumbs, crab meat, eggs, salad dressing, onions and lemon juice; mix well. Fill mushroom caps with filling. Sprinkle with cheese and bake at 375° for 15 minutes or until cheese is melted.

Crawdaddy Dip

1 can cream of shrimp soup
1 (8 oz.) pkg. cream cheese
1 handfull boiled crawdaddy meat

2 T. lemon juice
Dash of salt
2 shakes of garlic powder

Mix with beater. Be sure crawdaddy meat is cold.

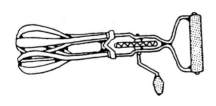

Betty's Caramel Puff Corn

1 C. brown sugar
½ C. margarine
¼ C. light corn syrup
¼ tsp. baking soda

1 tsp. vanilla
1 bag hull-less popcorn, Hilland Poppites

Boil for 2 minutes, stirring constantly, the brown sugar, margarine and light corn syrup. Remove from heat. Stir in baking soda and vanilla. Mix thoroughly and pour over popcorn. Bake at 250° for ½ hour. Cool slightly and break apart and store in plastic bags.

Cheese Ball

1 sharp cheddar cold pack
1 (8 oz.) pkg. Neutchatel diet cream cheese
Beau Monde seasoning

Onion flakes
Garlic salt
Chopped pecans, for top

Mix well, form into ball and refrigerate for a couple of hours. Put chopped pecans on top. Make day before.

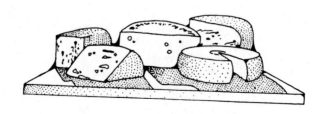

Curried Chicken Logs

2 (8 oz. ea.) pkgs. softened cream cheese
1 T. bottled steak sauce
½ tsp. curry powder
1½ C. minced cooked chicken
½ C. minced celery
2 T. chopped parsley
Parsley or almonds for garnish

Beat together cream cheese, steak sauce and curry powder. Blend in chicken, celery and parsley. Shape mixture into a 9-inch log. Wrap in plastic and chill. Use parsley or almonds to coat.

Deviled Eggs

4 slices bacon, crisply cooked, drained and crumbled
6 hard-cooked eggs
¼ C. mayonnaise or mayonnaise style salad dressing
1 tsp. prepared mustard
1 tsp. prepared horseradish
2 T. finely chopped green olives
Dash of salt
Dash of pepper

Halve hard-cooked eggs lengthwise; remove yolks and mash. Add mayonnaise, mustard, horseradish, olives, salt and pepper; mix well. Reserve 1 T. crumbled bacon for garnish; stir remaining bacon into deviled egg mixture. With small spoon, carefully fill center with yolk mixture. Garnish with bacon. Chill till serving time. Makes 12.

Kid Stopper Crawdaddy Bites

1 pkg. refrigerator butterflake rolls
8 oz. crawdaddy meat
1 (6 oz.) can water chestnuts, drained and diced
1 C. shredded Swiss cheese
½ C. mayonnaise
2 T. minced green onion, tops and bottoms
½ T. dill weed
1 tsp. lemon juice
Salt and pepper, to taste

Separate each roll into three layers. Place on ungreased baking sheet. Mix all other ingredients together and then spoon onto top of each roll. Bake at 350° for 15-20 minutes, checking to be sure they don't burn. May freeze before or after cooking. Yields: 36 pieces.

Carameled Popcorn

8 qts. popped corn, yellow works best
2 sticks margarine
½ C. white corn syrup
1 tsp. salt

2 C. brown sugar
1 tsp. burnt sugar flavoring
1 tsp. butter flavoring
½ tsp. baking soda
Peanuts

Bring to a slow boil, the margarine, white corn syrup, salt and 2 C. brown sugar. Cook for 5 minutes after mixture begins to boil. (Stir and watch, this will burn easily.) Then remove from heat and throughly stir in flavorings After flavorings are combined, add baking soda (adding soda will make it foam). Pour over popped corn and add peanuts. Stir together, then put in large cake pans. Put in a 250° oven for 1 hour, stirring every 15 minutes. Turn out on a cloth to cool. When completely cool, store in airtight containers.

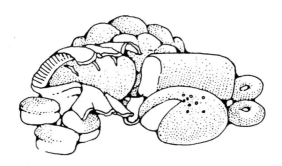

Cheese Bread Sticks

1 loaf frozen bread dough
4 T. margarine
2 tsp. beef bouillon
1 tsp. chicken bouillon

1 tsp. caraway seeds
2 tsp. poppy seeds
2 tsp. sesame seeds
½ lb. shredded cheese

Thaw bread dough and spread on greased 10 x 14-inch pan. Melt margarine and spread dough. Mix together bouillon and seed; spread over dough, then top with shredded cheese. Bake at 350° for 15-20 minutes. Cut in strips immediately.

Hog Heaven Ham Balls

2½ lbs. ground smoked ham
3 lbs. ground beef
4 eggs

2-3 C. crushed graham crackers
1 C. milk

SAUCE:
2 cans tomato soup
¾ C. vinegar

2¼ C. brown sugar
2 tsp. dry mustard

Combine ground meats, eggs, graham crackers and milk. Mix well and shape into 1-inch balls (makes 100-150). Combine ingredients for sauce and pour over meatballs. Bake at 300° for 2 hours. Serve warm or cold. Will freeze well.

Spinach Balls

2 pkgs. frozen chopped spinach, drained well
2 C. traditional Stove Top dressing
Salt and pepper

1 C. grated Parmesan cheese
6 beaten eggs
¾ C. softened butter

Mix together and make into balls. Bake at 350° for 15 minutes.

SALADS

Salads

Bean Salad 44
Broccoli Salad 48
Broccoli And Cauliflower Salad 40,44
Budget French Dressing 34
Cabbage Salad 38,43
Cauliflower Salad 37,39
Cheap Cabbage Salad 33
Cole Slaw Salad 45
Cranberry Jello Salad 37
Cranberry Salad Again 37
Cucumber Jello 48
Fruit Salad 45
Homemade Salad Dressing 35
Ice Box Slaw 44
Jello Vegetable Salad 47
Low Cost French Salad Dressing 35
Macaroni Salad 36
Marinated Carrots 38
Marinated Tomatoes 46
More Macaroni Salad 42
No Work Salad 46
Orange Layer Salad 47
Out-Of-Own Garden Salad 39
Potato Salad 39
Potato Salad Dressing 35
Raspberry Salad 33
Salad Dressing 34
7-Up Salad 48
Shell Macaroni Salad 36
The Slow Chicken Chicken Salad 46
Strawberry Salad 47
Summer Salad 43
Tart Sauerkraut Salad 44
The "Eat-Now!" Cauliflower & Pea Salad 40
Three Bean Salad 42
24 Hour Cabbage Salad 41
Vegetable Salad 45

- 32 -

Raspberry Salad

1 pkg. raspberry Jello
1 pkg. frozen raspberries, drained
2 (3 oz. ea.) pkgs. cream cheese
2 T. milk
1 C. whipped cream

Drain frozen raspberries and save juice. Add enough water to reserved juice to make 1 cup. Boil and add Jello. Beat cream cheese with milk until smooth. Gradually beat in hot gelatin. Chill until slightly thickened. Fold in raspberries and whipped cream. Chill until firm.

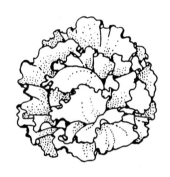

Cheap Cabbage Salad

3 C. sugar
2 C. vinegar
1 C. water
2 medium heads of cabbage
2 T. salt
1 bunch celery
2 green peppers, 1 can be red
Carrots
1 tsp. celery seed
1 tsp. mustard seed

Boil sugar, vinegar and water for 3 minutes; let cool. Shred cabbage; add salt and let stand for 1 hour. Squeeze out excess water. Grind celery, peppers, carrots, celery seed and mustard seed. Mix with drained cabbage and pour cooled liquid over cabbage. Will keep for 3 weeks in ice box in sealed jars. Makes 3 quarts.

Salad Dressing

½ C. sugar
½ C. vinegar
1 T. butter

1 beaten egg
1 C. sour cream

Bring sugar, vinegar and butter to a boil, then add egg and sour cream and boil until thick and smooth.

Salad Dressing

3 eggs, beaten
⅔ C. sugar
2 T. oleo or butter
⅓ C. vinegar

¼ tsp. salt
1 tsp. mustard (opt.)
Dash of pepper, if desired

Beat eggs, then add sugar, vinegar, salt and dash of pepper. Cook until thick; stir constantly. Add butter and beat well. Good for potato salad if thinned with some cream or Half & Half or better yet, mix this with about an equal amount of Miracle Whip or more. If making a small batch of salad you probably won't need all of it. Again, when mixing, taste frequently and season accordingly. You can always add more sugar, vinegar, salt, pepper, etc.

Budget French Dressing

1½ C. salad oil
1½ C. sugar
½ bottle catsup, sm. size

¼ C. vinegar
Salt and pepper

Beat together for 10 minutes and refrigerate.

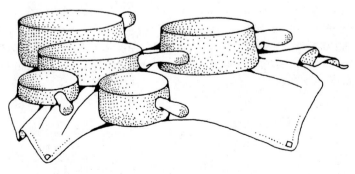

Homemade Salad Dressing

2 eggs, beaten
½ C. cream
½ C. vinegar

Pinch of salt
½-¾ C. sugar

Stir together and bring to a boil over low heat; stirring constantly. Cook until thick and then cool.

Potato Salad Dressing

¼ C. vinegar
¼ C. water
1 C. Miracle Whip
¼ C. sugar
¼ tsp. salt

2 tsp. prepared yellow mustard
2 eggs, beaten

Combine vinegar, water, sugar, salt and mustard. Bring to boil, lower heat gradually and stir eggs in easy. Cook slowly, stirring until slightly thickened, about 3 minutes or so. Cool some. Add Micacle Whip. Beat easy with spoon. Mix with potatoes or other salads.

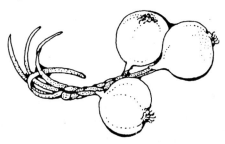

Low Cost French Salad Dressing

⅓ C. sugar
1 C. oil
¼ C. vinegar
½ tsp. salt or garlic salt
Celery seed

1 pinch of cloves
1 tsp. Worcestershire sauce
1 medium onion, minced
⅓ C. catsup

Add above ingredients as they come; mix well.

Macaroni Salad

1 lb. ring macaroni
1 lg. green pepper

4 shredded carrots
1 onion, chopped

DRESSING:
1 can sweetened condensed milk
1 C. sugar
1 C. vinegar

2 C. mayonnaise
1 tsp. salt
¼ tsp. pepper

Cook and cool ring macaroni, then add pepper, carrots and onion. For dressing: Combine condensed milk, sugar, vinegar, mayonnaise, salt and pepper. Pour dressing over macaroni mixture. Chill for 4 hours. Makes a large salad. It may seem soupy, but it absorbs as it sets.

Shell Macaroni Salad

1 lb. shell macaroni
4 carrots, grated
4 stalks celery, chopped
1 sm. onion, chopped
10 radishes, sliced
¾ C. vinegar

1 C. sugar
2 C. real mayonnaise
1 can Eagle Brand milk
1 tsp. salt
½ tsp. pepper

Cook macaroni until done. Drain and rinse with cold water, mix with chopped vegetables. Heat vinegar and sugar until sugar is dissolved. Cool, then add mayonnaise, Eagle Brand milk, salt and pepper. Beat until smooth and creamy. Pour over macaroni and vegetables and mix. Better if made day before.

Cranberry Jello Salad

2 C. hot water
2 pkgs. strawberry Jello
1 (14 oz.) can whole cranberries
1 C. cold water
½ C. sugar
½ C. nutmeats
2 apples, chopped fine

Mix Jello, sugar and add hot water; stir well. Add cold water and rest of ingredients. Chill until set.

Cauliflower Salad

1 head cauliflower, cut-up
10 oz. pkg. frozen peas, cooked and drained
2 carrots, grated
1 pkg. Good Seasons Italian dressing mix
½ C. diced celery with a little diced pepper
1 C. mayonnaise
1 C. sour cream

Combine all ingredients and cool.

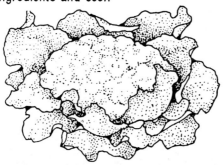

Cranberry Salad Again

2 C. ground cranberries
2 C. sugar
2 pkgs. lemon flavored gelatin
4 C. warm water
1 C. diced celery
1 C. broken nutmeats
1 orange, ground

Combine cranberries and sugar and let stand. Dissolve lemon gelatin and water; chill until partially set. Add all other ingredients and let stand until firm. Serves 10-12.

Marinated Carrots

7 C. carrots
2 C. celery
⅓ C. red pepper
⅓ C. green pepper
1 medium onion, chopped
1 C. sugar
¾ C. white vinegar

1 can tomato soup
1 tsp. yellow mustard, not dry
1 tsp. salt
½ tsp. pepper
1 tsp. Worcestershire sauce
¼ C lemon juice
½ tsp. anise seed

Cook carrots and celery until done, then drain. Run cold water to cool quickly. Cut up or grind peppers. Blend together sugar, vinegar, tomato soup, mustard, salt, pepper and Worcestershire sauce. Add carrots. Add lemon juice and ainse seed.

Cabbage Salad

1 head cabbage, shredded
1 onion, diced
1 green pepper, diced
⅓ C. vinegar
½ C. water
1 C. sugar

½ tsp. salt
2 stalks celery, diced
2-3 carrots, shredded
½ tsp. turmeric
¼ tsp. celery seed
¼ tsp. mustard seed

Combine vinegar, water, sugar, salt, turmeric, celery seed and mustard seed. Cook until it boils. Cool slightly and pour over combined vegetables. Keeps well in ice box for several days.

Potato Salad

6 lg. potatoes, boiled & cooked
4 hard-boiled eggs, cooled
1 sm. onion
Salt and pepper
Salad dressing

Dice or better yet, slice potatoes and then take a sharp knife and slice through several times until cut as desired. Cube eggs and onion; add to potatoes. Salt and pepper, to suit taste. You can add a dash of celery seed too. Now for the dressing, use a blend of ½ Miracle Whip, ½ homemade dressing or if in a hurry take the Miracle Whip and stir in some sugar and cream (milk or Half & Half may be used) until you have the right consistency and taste (you will have to sample it).

Cauliflower Salad

1 lg. head cauliflower
1 (10 oz.) jar stuffed salad olives
1 pt. Hellman's dressing
½ tsp. garlic powder
1 tsp. salt

Wash and break cauliflower into bite-sized pieces. Mix olives, dressing, garlic powder and salt; pour over cauliflower. Let stand overnight.

Out-Of-Our-Own Garden Salad

2 C. diced cauliflower
2 C. diced celery
2 C. shredded carrots
1 C. sliced radishes
1 C. drained peas
1 C. vinegar
¼ C salad oil
½ C. sugar
1 tsp. salt
¼ tsp. pepper

Mix all vegetables together. Mix vinegar, oil, sugar, salt and pepper. Fold into vegetables and refrigerate. Can be made 2 days ahead of time for use.

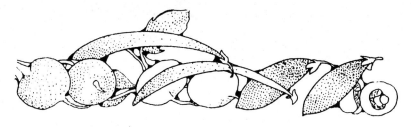

Broccoli And Cauliflower Salad

2 C. chopped broccoli
2 C. chopped cauliflower
1 C. chopped pepper, half red
1 C. celery
1 C. chopped & seeded tomatoes
1 C. cubed cheddar cheese
6 green onions, chopped
1 C. mayonnaise
1 C. sour cream
1 T. lemon juice
1 T. powdered sugar

Combine broccoli, cauliflower, peppers, celery, tomatoes, cheese and onions. Blend together mayonnaise, sour cream, lemon juice and powdered sugar. Pour over vegetables and toss until well coated. This makes a large salad and will serve 15-20 people.

The "Eat-Now" Cauliflower And Pea Salad

3 stalks celery, chopped
1 sm. onion, grated
1 C. mayonnaise
1½ tsp. seasoned salt
¾ tsp. milk or more
20 oz. bag frozen peas, thawed
1 head cauliflower, sm. pieces

Mix chopped celery, grated onion, thawed peas and a head of cauliflower (cut in small pieces). Add mayonnaise, salt and milk; let marinate for several hours.

Ice Box Slaw

1 medium head cabbage, shredded
1 tsp. salt
2 carrots, grated

2 stalks celery, chopped
½ green pepper, chopped

DRESSING:
1 C. vinegar
½ C. water
1½ C. sugar

1 tsp. celery seed
1 tsp. mustard seed

Mix shredded cabbage and salt; let stand for 1 hour and drain liquid. Add rest of vegetables. Boil dressing ingredients for 1 minute. Cool and pour over vegetables mixture. Refrigerate.

24 Hour Cabbage Salad

1 head cabbage, shredded
1 green pepper, chopped fine
½ C. vinegar
2 C. sugar

1 tsp. salt
1 tsp. mustard seed
1 tsp. celery seed

Mix all together and let stand for 24 hours in ice box.

Three Bean Salad

1 can green beans
1 can yellow wax beans
1 can red kidney beans
1 green pepper, chopped
1 medium onion, chopped
¾ C. celery, chopped

¾ C. sugar
½ C. oil
½ C vinegar
1 tsp. salt
1 tsp. pepper

Drain beans and add remaining vegetables. Combine sugar, oil, vinegar, salt and pepper; pour over the beans. Let stand overnight.

More Macaroni Salad

1 pt. mayonnaise
1 C. vinegar
1½ C. sugar
1 can Eagle Brand milk

1 lb. twist macaroni
1 green pepper, chopped
2 grated carrots
1 chopped onion

Cook macaroni according to directions on package; drain. Stir mayonnaise, vinegar, sugar and milk until smooth. Fold in macaroni and vegetables. Cover tightly and refrigerate for 3-4 hours or overnight.

Cabbage Salad

1 head of cabbage
1 onion
1 red pepper
1 green pepper

1 C. vinegar
1 C. sugar
Celery seed

Shred cabbage, onion and peppers. Salt down and let set at least 2 hours, then drain. Boil vinegar, sugar and celery seed. Cool and pour over cabbage. This will keep a long time in ice box.

Summer Salad

1 head cauliflower
1 bunch broccoli
1 red onion

⅓ C. sugar
⅓ C. mayonnaise
⅓ C. oil

Wash and cut into pieces the cauliflower, broccoli and onion. Mix sugar, mayonnaise and oil. Pour over vegetables and marinate overnight.

Broccoli And Cauliflower Salad

1 head cauliflower
1 bunch green onions
1 bunch broccoli
1 C. raw frozen peas
2 C. salad dressing

Splash of buttermilk
2 tsp. salt
2 C. sour cream
3 tsp. garlic

Wash and cut into pieces the cauliflower, onion, broccoli and peas. Mix salad dressing, buttermilk, salt, sour cream and garlic. Mix well with vegetables.

Tart Sauerkraut Salad

1 (16 oz.) can sauerkraut
1 C. chopped celery
½ C. chopped onion
1 chopped green pepper
1 sm. jar chopped pimentos

1 C. sugar
¼ tsp. salt
Dash of pepper
¼ C. white vinegar

Drain sauerkraut and chop fine. Mix remaining ingredients and chill thoroughly. Serve with a slotted spoon to eliminate juice. Place each serving on lettuce. Refrigerate in airtight container.

Bean Salad

2 C. cooked dry beans, drained
1 C. sliced sweet pickles
1 diced onion
Salt and pepper

1 C. vinegar
1 C. sugar
1 egg
1 tsp. cornstarch

Cool dry beans. Mix vinegar, sguar, egg and cornstarch; cook until thick. Cool and pour over beans, pickles and onion. Mix together and add salt and pepper, to taste.

Vegetable Salad

1 can whole kernel corn
1 can French-style green beans
1 can peas
1 C. chopped celery
1 C. chopped onion
1 C. chopped green pepper
¾ C. vinegar
1 C. sugar
1 tsp. salt
1 T. water

Drain corn, beans and peas. Mix with remaining vegetables. Boil vinegar, sugar, salt and water. Let cool and pour over vegetables. Let stand overnight. Will keep at least 2 weeks in ice box.

Fruit Salad

1 lg. can pineapple chunks, drained
1 can peach pie filling
3-4 sliced bananas
1 can mandarin oranges, drained
1 carton fresh strawberries, thawed or fresh

Mix together and chill. Can be made the night before. Bananas, will not turn dark.

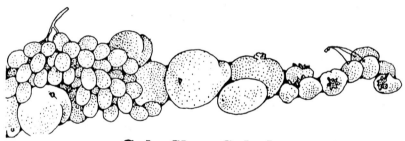

Cole Slaw Salad

1 head cabbage
1 sm. onion
½ green pepper
1 carrot
1 C. Miracle Whip
¼ C. oil
¾ C. sugar
¼ C. vinegar
Dash of salt

Grate cabbage, onion, pepper and carrot. Mix together and top with blend of Miracle Whip, oil, sugar, vinegar and salt.

No Work Salad

1 can chunk pineapple, drained
2 sm. cans mandarin oranges, drained
1 can peach pie filling

1 C. sliced bananas or any other fruit desired

Mix entire contents together. Can be kept over day or 2 as acid in peach pie filling prevents bananas from turning dark.

Marinated Tomatoes

4-6 tomatoes, quartered
1 onion, sliced
1 green pepper, sliced
1 cucumber, sliced

1 C. oil
1 C. vinegar
1 C. sugar
Salt and pepper

Mix oil, vinegar, sugar, salt and pepper. Pour over vegetables and let marinate in ice box at least ½ day.

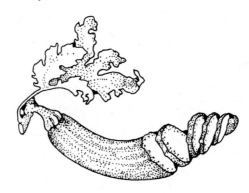

The Slow Chicken Chicken Salad

3 C. cubed chicken
1 C. diced celery
1 tsp. salt

3 hard-boiled eggs
3 sweet pickles
Mayonnaise, as desired

Mix all together and add mayonnaise as desired for moistness. Serve on lettuce leaf and garnish with olives.

Orange Layer Salad

1 pkg. orange gelatin
1 C. boiling water
1 sm. can mandarin oranges,
   drained
1 sliced banana

Juice from oranges plus cold water
   to make ¾ C.
1 C. whipped cream or Dream
   Whip

Dissolve Jello in hot water. Add juice and cold water. Chill until slightly thick. Fold in whipped cream, oranges and banana slices. Put in Jello mold and chill till firm. Before serving, remove Jello from mold. Salad will have set in layers. Can be garnished with whipped cream, coconut and fruit.

Strawberry Salad

3 sm. boxes strawberry Jello
3 C. boiling water
2 (10 oz.) boxes frozen strawberries

1 (12½ oz.) can crushed pineapple
3 lg. bananas, sliced
1 C. dairy sour cream

Dissolve Jello in boiling water. Add strawberries; stir until thawed. Add crushed pineapple and bananas. Pour ½ of mixture into 9 x 13-inch pan and chill until firm. Spread evenly with sour cream. Pour remaining gelatin mixture on top and chill till firm.

Jello Vegetable Salad

2 (3 oz. ea.) pkgs. lemon Jello
2 C. hot water
1¼ C. mayonnaise or 1 C.
   mayonnaise & ¼ C. Cool Whip
1 C. cottage cheese

¾ C. finely chopped celery
1 C. finely chopped or shredded
   carrots
2 T. chopped onion
1 chopped green pepper

Dissolve Jello in the hot water and let set until slightly thickened. Add remaining ingredients and refrigerate.

Cucumber Jello

1 box lemon or lime Jello
1¼ C. boiling water
1 C. shredded cucumbers
1 onion, shredded
1 T. vinegar
½ tsp. salt

Dissolve Jello in boiling water and cool. Add cucumbers, onion, vinegar and salt. Refrigerate.

Broccoli Salad

1 pkg. chopped frozen broccoli
¾ C. green olives
1 sm. onion, chopped
3 hard cooked eggs, chopped
½ C. mayonnaise

Cook broccoli according to package directions. Drain and cool. Add remaining ingredients. (Note: This salad may be made a day ahead. Very good!)

7-Up Salad

1 C. applesauce
½ C. orange juice
1 pkg. lime Jello
1 sm. bottle 7-Up

Heat applesauce and orange juice. Dissolve Jello in it and cool. Add 7-Up and refrigerate.

SOUPS

SOUPS

Broccoli-Cauliflower soup 51
Hamburger Vegetable Soup 53
Hard Times Potato Soup 54
No-Left-Overs Beef Stew 52
Real Cheap Vegetable Beef Barley Soup 53
Ribbles For Soup 55
The Cat's Meow Hamburger Soup 52
Vegetable Beef Soup 54
Vegetable Chowder 55
Wash Day Fish Chowder 51

Broccoli-Cauliflower Soup

1 lb. fresh broccoli, cut in small pieces
1 lb. fresh cauliflower, cut in small pieces
2 chicken bouillon cubes
½ C. margarine
1 medium onion, chopped
½ C. flour
4 C. milk
2 C. shredded cheddar cheese

Boil broccoli, cauliflower and chicken bouillon cubes in a 3 quart saucepan with just enough water to cover, until vegetables are just tender, approximately 3 minutes. Meanwhile, *saute* ½ C. margarine and 1 medium chopped onion in a ½ quart saucepan. Add ½ C. flour and mix. Add 4 C. milk and cook over medium heat until thickened. Add mixture to vegetables, after they have been boiled. Add 2 C. shredded cheddar cheese. Heat until cheese melts through. Season with salt and pepper and serve. Yield: Serves 4 to 6.

Wash Day Fish Chowder

1 C. carrots
2 C. potatoes
½ C. onion
1 C. celery
2-3 lbs. fillet fish

Boil cut-up fish pieces until done; strain. Save fish water for broth. In broth boil diced carrots, potatoes, onion and celery. Add salt, pepper, allspice, bay leaf and chicken broth or bouillon. Add medium white sauce.

No Left Overs Beef Stew

2 lbs. beef stew meat or a roast, cut into 1-inch cubes
4 medium onions, sliced
¼ C. soy sauce
¾ tsp. salt
½ tsp. pepper
4-6 lg. diced potatoes
4 lg. carrots, cut into chunks
1 celery (opt.)
3 T. flour
Water

Put sliced onions and meat in bottom of small roaster. Pour enough water over this to cover well. Add soy sauce. Mix flour, salt and pepper together. Pour over water and mix well. May be lumpy but these will cook out. Bake covered for 1 hour at 350°. Add carrots and celery. Bake for another ½ hour, then add potatoes. Bake for another hour or until done. Add more water if necessary. If more water is added, add some additional flour to keep broth thick. Makes 6 to 8 servings.

The Cat's Meow Hamburger Soup

1½ lbs. hamburger
½ C. chopped onion
2 C. tomato juice or tomatoes
1¼ C. diced potatoes
1 C. diced celery
6 C. water
¼ C. rice, uncooked
1¼ C. diced carrots
2 tsp. salt
¼ tsp. black pepper

Brown hamburger and onion. Place in large kettle. Add remaining ingredients and simmer 1 hour. Serve.

Real Cheap Vegetable Beef Barley Soup

3 T. salad oil
2 lbs. beef chuck, cut into ¾-inch cubes (I use stew meat)
2 C. chopped onions
1 tsp. minced garlic
½ tsp. thyme
½ tsp. marjoram
6 C. water
2 cans (about 14 oz. ea.) beef broth
1½ C. diced carrots
¾ C. diced celery
1½ tsp. salt
½ tsp. freshly ground pepper
3 C. diced potatoes
¾ C. barley

In large pot, heat oil over medium high heat. Add meat and cook, stirring occasionally, until browned on all sides. Add onions, garlic, thyme and marjoram. Cook stirring, 10 minutes more. Add water, beef broth, carrots, celery, barley*, salt and pepper. Bring to a boil; reduce heat and simmer uncovered 30-40 minutes, until potatoes are tender. (*If using quick barley, add with the potatoes.) Makes 14 cups, 225 calories per cup.

Hamburger Vegetable Soup

1 lb. hamburger
½ C. chopped onion
2 C. raw cubed potatoes
2 C. raw cubed carrots
½ C. chopped celery
¼ C. uncooked rice
2 C. tomato juice
Add 1 qt. or more water, as desired

Brown hamburger and onion. Add rest of ingredients and simmer 1 hour.

Hard Times Potato Soup

6-8 lg. potatoes
1 lg. onion
4 stalks celery
¼ lb. butter

1 C. cold milk
1 egg and 1 C. cold milk, beaten together

Cut-up and cook vegetables until well done. Add butter. Mash with potato masher and add 1 C. cold milk. Stir and add egg and milk mixture. Heat until hot but do not boil. Add salt and pepper, to taste.

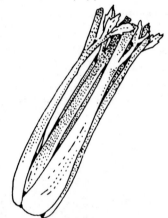

Vegetable Beef Soup

2 T. vegetable oil
1 lb. boneless beef chuck, 1" cubes
1 C. onion
3 T. flour
1 (14 oz.) can beef broth

1 (16 oz.) can whole tomatoes
½ tsp. celery salt
1½ C. uncooked macaroni
1 C. frozen peas
1 C. frozen corn

Heat oil over high heat in 5 quart saucepan. Add meat and brown on all sides about 5 minutes. Reduce heat to moderate, add onions and cook 5-7 minutes, stirring several times, until soft. Stir in flour. Whisk in beef broth and gently scrape bottom of pot to loosen brown particles. Stir in tomatoes, celery, salt and 3 C. water. Bring to a boil, reduce heat, cover and simmer for 45 minutes. Add macaroni, corn and peas. Increase heat to moderate, cover and boil 20 minutes, stirring occasionally to keep pasta from sticking. Makes 8 cups.

Ribbles For Soup

1 egg
Dash of salt
2 C. flour

Ribbles are thin strands of dough used to thicken soups. They may be as thick or as fine as you like. To make: Beat the egg and work the flour into egg by rubbing the mixture with the fingers to desired thinness. Add ribbles to soup 10 minutes before serving and simmer.

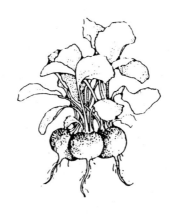

Vegetable Chowder

2 C. diced potatoes
¾ C. diced onions
½ C. diced celery
½ C. diced carrots
2½ C. boiling water
2 tsp. salt
4 T. flour
4 T. butter, melted

2 C. milk
½ tsp. pepper
½ tsp. dried mustard
½ T. minced parsley
¼ lb. grated cheddar cheese
1 C. canned tomatoes with pinch soda in them
¼ C. sugar, to suit taste
1 can creamed corn

Put potatoes, onions, celery and carrots in boiling water with salt. Cook until tender. In saucepan mix flour and butter together. Add milk and mix well. Add pepper, mustard, parsley and cheese. Pour cooked vegetables and sauce together. Add tomatoes, sugar and creamed corn. Heat well and serve.

- 56 -

MAIN DISHES

MAIN DISHES

Au Gratin Cheese Potatoes 65
Barbecue Beef Sandwiches 94
Barbecued Brisket 83
Baked Chicken (Or other Fowl) & Rice 74
Baked Corn 64
Baked Fish 62
Baked Pork Chops 76
Baked Swiss Steak 83
Barbecued Venison 71
Bean Casserole 89
Beef And Potato Loaf 92
Beef Ribs 84
Breakfast Egg-Cheese Casserole 70
Cabbage Dish 63
Carrot Casserole 67
Cheese Crisp Baked Chicken 71
Cheese Scalloped Carrots 68
Cheesy Meat Loaf 78
Chicken Dumplings 73
Chicken-Noodle Scallop 75
Chicken Sandwich Filling 65
Chicken Stew 70
Corn Casserole 69
Corn Pudding 63
Crunch Top Potatoes 64
Eggs Brunch (Make Day Before) 93
Egg-Sausage Casserole 93
Everyday Meat Loaf 61
Fast Meat Balls 88
Flank Steak 86
French Toast Casserole 90
Fried Green Tomatoes 65
Garden Pepper Steak 85
Gimmie More Meat Loaf 79
Good Times Rice 'N Hamburger Casserole 91
Green Pepper Steak 80,87
Ham Balls 62

MAIN DISHES-CONTINUED

Ham And Egg Breakfast 92
Ham Logs 75
Helen's Meat Balls 81
Herb Chicken 75
Layered Chicken 73
Mama's Corn Fritters 63
Meatballs 89
Meat Loaf 79,81
Meat Noodles 78
Nap Time Chicken on Sunday 69
No Peek Beef Stew 69
Oven Crisp Chicken 72
Oven Fried Chicken 72
Payday Herbed Chicken 74
Payday Meatballs 78
Pig Pie 90
Pork Chops 77
Pork Chop Wow 77
Raised Meatballs 88
Real Good Swiss Steak 84
Rolled Meat Loaf 80
Salisbury Steak 86
Sauerkraut Casserole 68
Sausage Casserole 91
Scalloped Corn 64
Sharon's Meatloaf 76
Scalloped Potatoes 67
Spaghetti Pie 61
Sweet Potatoes 66
Sweet Sour Steak 87
Swiss Steak 85
Time To Splurge Egg Brunch 94
The Boy Filler Scalloped Cabbage 66
Three Bean Casserole 82
Washday Meat Balls 82
Whatever Casserole 77

- 60 -

Everyday Meat Loaf

2 beaten eggs
¾ C. milk
½ C. fine dry bread crumbs
¼ C. finely chopped onion
2 T. snipped parsley (opt.)
1 tsp. salt

½ tsp. ground sage
1/8 tsp. pepper
1½ lbs. ground beef
¼ C. catsup
2 T. brown sugar
1 tsp. dry mustard

In bowl, combine eggs and milk. Stir in bread crumbs and onion, parsley, salt, sage and pepper. Add ground beef; mix well. Shape meat mixture into desired shape. Pat mixture into 8 x 4 x 2-inch loaf pan. Bake meat loaf, uncovered, in 350° oven (allow 1¼ hours). Spoon off excess fat. Combine catsup, brown sugar and dry mustard. Spread over meat loaf, return to oven and bake 10 minutes more. Makes 6 servings.

Spaghetti Pie

6 oz. spaghetti
⅓ C. grated Parmesan cheese
1 C. (8 oz.) cottage cheese
½ C. chopped onion
1 C. (8 oz.) can tomatoes, cut-up
1 tsp. sugar
½ tsp. garlic salt
2 T. butter

2 well beaten eggs
1 lb. ground beef or bulk pork
   sausage
¼ C. chopped green pepper
1 (6 oz.) can tomato juice
1 tsp. dried oregano, crushed
½ C. (2 oz.) shredded mozzarella
   cheese

Cook the spaghetti according to package directions; drain. (Should have about 3 C. spaghetti.) Stir butter into hot spaghetti. Stir in Parmesan cheese and eggs. Form spaghetti crust. In skillet cook ground beef or pork sausage, onion and green pepper until vegetables are tender and meat is browned. Drain off excess fat. Stir in undrained tomatoes, tomato paste, sugar, oregano and garlic salt; heat through. Turn meat mixture into spaghetti crust. Bake, uncovered in 350° oven for 20 minutes. Sprinkle the mozzarella cheese atop. Bake 5 minutes longer or until cheese melts. Makes 6 servings.

Baked Fish

1 lb. fish filets
2 T. lemon juice
¼ C. butter
½ C. cracker crumbs

1 sm. can mushrooms
½ C. chopped onion
2 T. parsley
4-5 slices bacon

Lay the fish in casserole and sprinkle with the lemon juice. Melt the butter; add cracker crumbs. Mix and pour on fish. Add the mushrooms, onion and parsley. Cover with bacon and bake at 400° for 30-35 minutes. Bake uncovered and bast every 10 minutes.

Ham Balls

3 lbs. ground ham
1 lb. ground beef
1 lb. ground pork
3 .C graham crackers, crushed

2 C. milk
¼ tsp. pepper
3 eggs
1 tsp. salt

SAUCE:
1 C. water
1 C. brown sugar
1 tsp. mustard

1 C. catsup
¾ C. vinegar

Mix well and shape into balls. Cook in sauce. For sauce: Boil and pour over ham balls. Bake at 325° for 90 minutes. Baste during baking. Serves 32.

Cabbage Dish

1 head cabbage
2 C. medium white sauce
1 lg. cream cheese
Buttered bread crumbs

Chop and cook cabbage until tender. Drain and put in baking dish. Prepare white sauce and melt cream cheese in it. Pour sauce with melted cream cheese over cabbage. Top with buttered bread crumbs. Bake at 350° until it looks hot and bubbly.

Mama's Corn Fritters

1 C. canned corn
1 egg, well beaten
⅔ C. flour
2¾ tsp. baking powder
1 tsp. salt
Few grains of pepper

Mix ingredients in order. Drop by spoonfuls in deep fat. Fry until golden brown.

Corn Pudding

2 C. raw corn, cut and milked from ears
⅔ C. heavy cream
1 T. flour
Pinch of salt
Pinch of pepper

Mix well. Pour into greased 4 C. casserole. Bake 1 hour at 350°.

Baked Corn

2 eggs
1 T. flour
1 T. sugar
8 soda crackers, put on top

1 can cream style corn
1 T. melted butter
½ tsp. salt
½ C. milk

Beat eggs; add corn and rest of ingredients in order given. Crush soda crackers and put on top. Bake in greased casserole for 30 minutes at 375° and 30 minutes more at 350° until golden brown.

Crunch Top Potatoes

6 T. butter
3-4 lg. baking potatoes, pared and cut in ½-inch crosswise slices

¾ C. crushed cornflakes
1 C. shredded cheddar cheese
1 tsp. paprika
1 tsp. salt

Melt butter in 15½ × 10½-inch pan; like flat cookies or jelly roll pan. Add single layer of sliced potatoes, turn once in the melted fat or butter. Mix the crushed cornflakes, cheese, salt and paprika. Sprinkle over the top. Bake at 350° for ½ hour or until done and tops are crisp.

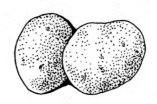

Scalloped Corn

1 C. shredded cheddar cheese
¼ C. milk
1 can cream style corn
2 T. sugar
2 T. flour

2 T. melted oleo
2 eggs
1 tsp. salt
1 medium pepper, chopped
1 can pimento, chopped

Grease the casserole and mix all ingredients together. Bake at 350° for 1 hour.

Au Gratin Cheese Potatoes

Cook 8-9 medium potatoes with peeling. When cold, peel and grate. Heat 1 C. Half and Half, ½ C. butter and 1 tsp. salt. Pour over potatoes in greased 9 x 13-inch loaf pan. Top with 8 oz. mild cheddar cheese. Bake 40-45 minutes in 350° oven.

Fried Green Tomatoes

BATTER:
1 C. cornmeal
½ C. flour
2 tsp. baking powder
1 tsp. salt, or less

1 T. sugar
Pinch of pepper
1 C. milk

6-8 green tomatoes

To fry: Cut tomatoes into ¼-inch slices. Dip in batter and fry in deep fat, drain and serve.

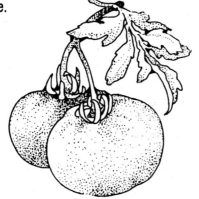

Chicken Sandwich Filling

1½ C. chopped chicken
¼ C. chopped pickle
1 tsp. Worcestershire sauce

⅓ C. undiluted cream of chicken soup
¼ tsp. celery, salt or powder

Mix together all ingredients. Makes enough for 6 sandwiches.

Sweet Potatoes

1 butternut squash
1 C. brown sugar
¼ C. water

¼ C. butter
½ tsp. salt

Pare squash and cut into chunks. Place in buttered casserole. Make syrup of brown sugar, water, butter and salt. Pour over squash. Cover and bake at 325° approximately 1 hour, basting occasionally. Uncover last half of baking time.

The Boy Filler Scalloped Cabbage

Cabbage
Salt and pepper
Flour

Grated American cheese
Milk

Layer grated cabbage into casserole in layers. Sprinkle flour, salt, pepper and grated American cheese over each layer. Barely cover iwth milk or Half and Half. Put cracker crumbs on top. Bake at 350° for 1 hour or until done.

Scalloped Potatoes

3 T. butter
2 T. flour
¾ tsp. salt
¼ tsp. pepper

3½ C. milk
6 C. thinly sliced potatoes
1 C. chopped onion
1 C. chopped ham (opt.)

Melt butter; add and blend flour, salt, pepper and onion. Gradually add milk. Cook until smooth and thick, stirring constantly. Add potatoes and ham. Cover and simmer 7 minutes. Pour into greased dish or roaster. Bake uncovered at 350° until tender, about 35 minutes. They will have a golden brown crust.

Carrot Casserole

4½ C. carrots
1 stick butter
½ lb. American cheese

1 onion, chopped
1½ C cornflakes

Parboil carrots until tender. Melt butter and grate cheese. Layer portions, cheese, butter, carrots in a casserole and repeat with cornflakes on top. Bake at 325° for about 1 hour until cheese melts.

Sauerkraut Casserole

5 strips bacon, fried and crumbled
1 sm. onion, chopped
1 C. brown sugar

2 lbs. sauerkraut
1 can tomatoes, drained

Combine and bake 1 hour at 350°.

Cheese Scalloped Carrots

12 sliced carrots
1 minced onion
¼ C. butter
¼ C. flour
1 tsp. salt
¼ tsp. dry mustard

2 C. milk
1/8 tsp. pepper
¼ tsp. celery salt
½ lb. sharp cheese, grated
3 C. buttered soft bread crumbs

Cook carrots until barely tender. Cook onion in butter. Slowly add flour, salt and mustard, then milk, pepper and celery salt. In a 2 quart casserole arrange a layer of carrots, then a layer of cheese, repeat ending wiht a layer of carrots. Pour on sauce, top with crumbs. Bake at 350° for 35-40 minutes. Serves 8.

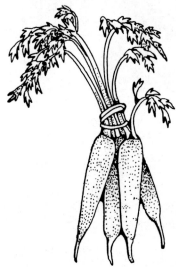

Corn Casserole

1 beaten egg
2/3 C. milk
1 can cream style corn
1 can whole corn
1 stick melted butter
2 T. sugar

Salt and pepper, to taste
1/4 C. chopped onion
1/4 C. chopped green pepper
1 sm. jar pimentos
1 C. cracker crumbs
1 C. grated cheese

Mix in order given. Bake in greased casserole at 350° for 1 hour.

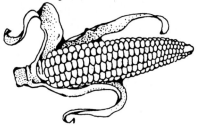

Nap Time Chicken On Sunday

1 can mushroom soup
1 can celery soup
1 pkg. onion soup mix

1 can raw rice, Uncle Ben's converted rice
Raw chicken

Heat soups and rice together. Pour into large buttered casserole. Lay pieces of raw chicken on top and sprinkle with onion soup mix. Cover tightly and bake 2 hours and 15 minutes at 325°.

No Peek Beef Stew

1 1/2 lbs. stew meat
6 sm. potatoes
6 sm. carrots
6 sm. onions
1/2 C. tomato juice
1/2 C. water

1 beef bouillon cube
1 1/2 tsp. salt
1 tsp. sugar
1/2 tsp. pepper
3 T. minute tapioca

Put first 4 ingredients in Dutch oven or large casserole. Combine spices and tapioca and sprinkle over vegetables and meat. Heat water, juice and cube. Pour over all. Cover and bake 5 hours at 250°. Do not peek!

Breakfast Egg-Cheese Casserole

6 slices bread
2 C. smoked ham
8 oz. sliced cheese

5 beaten eggs
2½ C. milk
⅓ C. melted butter

Remove crust and line 9 x 13-inch glass pan with bread. Put chopped ham on bread. Place cheese slices over ham. Mix eggs and milk; pour over rest of ingredients. Drizzle butter over all. Refrigerate for 12 hours. Bake at 350° for 1 hour. Let stand for 10 minutes before serving.

Chicken Stew

1 broiler-fryer chicken
2 chicken bouillon cubes
4 potatoes, scrubbed & peeled
3 medium onions, chopped
4 carrots, sliced crosswise

1 bag or bunch spinach
1½ C. skim milk
2 tsp. salt
½ tsp. pepper
¼ tsp. Tabasco sauce (opt.)

Cook chicken in water until tender, save broth, remove chicken from bone (discard skin, fat and bone). Cook vegetables in broth with 2 bouillon cubes added (except spinach) until tender. Mash potatoes; add chicken meat to broth and vegetables. Add spinach, milk, salt and Tabasco sauce. Heat through, but do not overcook spinach. Serves 6 to 8.

Barbecued Venison

1 lb. venison
1 medium onion, chopped
½ C. celery, chopped
2 T. butter or margarine
1 C. ketchup
1 C. water
2 T. brown sugar
2 T. vinegar
3 T. Worcestershire sauce
¼ C. lemon juice
Salt
Pepper

Dredge venison in flour and brown. Place in baking dish. Saute' onion and celery in butter until tender. Add remaining ingredients, stir and cook on medium until flavors are well blended, about 15 mintues. Pour over venison and bake at 350° for 1½ hours.

Cheese Crisp Baked Chicken

2 C. bread crumbs, older the better
1 C. shredded cheese
2 T. chopped parsley
1 tsp. salt
¼ tsp. pepper
½ tsp. garlic salt
1 frying chicken, cut in serving pieces
¾ C. melted butter

Combine crumbs, cheese, parsley and seasonings. Dip chicken in butter and then in crumb mixture. Arrange in single layer in shallow baking dish with meat side of pieces up. Pour remaining crumbs over top. Drizzle any remaining butter over all of chicken. Bake at 350° for 1-1¼ hours. Yield: 4 servings.

Oven Crisp Chicken

¼ C. butter
1 C. potato flakes
2 T. dry onion flakes
½ tsp. chili powder

¼ C. Parmesan cheese
1 egg
2 T. milk

Melt the butter and pour into cake pan or cookie sheet. Salt the chicken pieces and dip the chicken in mixture of 1 egg and 2 T. milk. Mix all the dry ingredients together. Roll the chicken in potato mixture. Place skin side down in the buttered pan. Bake at 350° for 1½ hours. Turn chicken halfway through cooking time.

Oven Fried Chicken

1 frying chicken, cut-up
1½ C. poultry stuffing mix
2 T. Parmesan cheese

½ clove garlic, crushed
¼ C. butter

Whirl the stuffing mix in blender or crush into crumbs with rolling pin. Stir in grated cheese. Add crushed garlic to butter and melt. Dip chicken pieces in the garlic butter and coat with the stuffing and cheese mixture. Bake in a buttered casserole at 350° for 1 hour. (You may want to remove the skin.) Serves 2-4.

Layered Chicken

8 slices day old bread
2 C. diced cooked chicken
½ C. chopped onion
½ C. green pepper
½ C. finely chopped celery
½ C. mayonnaise
¾ tsp. salt
Dash of pepper
2 slightly beaten eggs
1½ C. milk
2 cans cream mushroom soup, condensed
½ C. shredded sharp American cheese

Butter 2 slices bread, cut in ½-inch cubes and set aside. Cut remaining bread in 1-inch cubes. Place half of unbuttered cubes in bottom of 9-inch baking dish. Combine chicken, vegetables, mayonnaise and seasonings. Spoon over bread cubes. Sprinkle remaining unbuttered cubes over chicken mixture. Combine eggs and milk pour over all. Cover and chill 1 hour or better overnight. Spoon soup over top. Sprinkle wiht buttered cubes. Bake in 325° oven for 1 hour or until set. Sprinkle cheese over top last few minutes of baking. Makes 6 to 8 servings.

Chicken Dumplings

1 fried chicken, cut in pieces

DUMPLINGS:
2 C. flour
2 tsp. baking powder
½ tsp. salt
Water

Fry chicken in skillet until brown. Make a thin gravy and then add to the chicken and simmer until done. Add the dumplings last. For dumplings: Mix the flour, baking powder and salt and enough water for stiff dough. Drop by spoonfuls on top of pieces of fried chicken and gravy in skillet. Cover with lid and do not take lid off. Simmer for 15 minutes.

Payday Herbed Chicken

2½ lbs. chicken, cut-up
¼ C. flour
2 T. oil
1 C. dry white wine
1 C. sliced mushrooms

1 tsp. salt
1 tsp. tarragon
1 tsp. thyme
1 tsp. chopped chives (opt.)
¼ tsp. pepper

Coat chicken with flour. In 12-inch skillet over medium heat in hot oil, cook chicken until brown on all sides, about 15 mintes. Add remaining ingredients and heat to boiling. Reduce heat to low. Cover skillet and cook 30 minutes or until chicken is fork tender. Good over rice. Yield: 4 servings. 300 calories per serving.

Baked Chicken (Or Other Fowl) And Rice

9 chicken breasts
2 pkgs. Uncle Ben's long grain wild rice
1 can cream of chicken soup

⅔ can whole milk, to thin soup
Pimento for color
Paprika

Roll chicken in mixture of flour, salt, pepper and paprika. Brown slowly in hot oil. Mix soup, milk and pimento together until smooth. Cook rice according to directions on package. Mix cooked rice, pemento and soup. Pour in greased shallow baking dish. Lay browned chicken on top of rice mixture. Cover and bake at 325° for 1 hour. Uncover and bake ½ hour more at 350°.

Chicken-Noodle Scallop

1 can cream of chicken soup
½ C. milk
1¾ C. frozen peas
1½ C. cooked noodles

1½ C. diced cooled chicken
¼ C. chopped onion
¼ tsp. paprika
Dash pepper

Mix soup and milk, bring to a boil. Remove from heat. Add peas, noodles, onion, chicken, peprika and pepper; mix well. Pour into 1½ quart baking dish; top with ¼ C. buttered bread crumbs. Bake at 350° for 35-40 minutes. Serves 4

Herb Chicken

1 can cream of chicken soup
1 can water chestnuts
2 T. green onion
2 T. ground pepper

¾ C. white wine
1 sm. can mushrooms
¼ tsp. thyme
3 T. butter, melted

Brown chicken and place in pan. Mix ingredients and pour over and bake at 350° for 1 hour.

Ham Logs

2 lbs. ground beef
2 lbs. ground ham
1 lb. ground pork
4 eggs
1 C. oatmeal

1 C. milk
½ C. brown sugar
1 C. water
1 T. mustard

Combine all meat, eggs, oatmeal and milk, then shape into logs. Mix sugar, water and dry mustard. Pour over logs and bake slowly for 2 hours.

Baked Pork Chops

6 pork chops
1 can cream style corn
1 egg, beaten
2 T. butter, melted

2 T. green pepper (opt.)
½ C. cracker crumbs
2 T. chopped onion
1 tsp. sugar

Place browned and seasoned chops in pan or roaster. Mix together the next 7 ingredients and put on top of pork chops. Bake 1 hour in a slow oven, 325°. Serve with baked potatoes and a tossed green salad.

Sharon's Meatloaf

2 lbs. ground chuck
1 egg
1 tsp. salt
¼ tsp. pepper
½ tsp. leaf basil
½ tsp. thyme
¼ C. catsup

2 tsp. prepared mustard
1½ C. bread crumbs
2 beef bouillon cubes in 1 C. boiling water
½ C. finely chopped celery
½ C. chopped onion
1 C. shredded cheddar or Swiss cheese

Mix all ingredients and bake at 375° for 60-70 minutes.

Pork Chops Wow

8 pork chops
2 tsp. salt
½ tsp. pepper
8 thin onion slices
8 green pepper rings
8 T. uncooked instant rice
1 (16 oz.) can stewed tomatoes

In large skillet brown chops over medium heat. Sprinkle with salt and pepper. Top each with 1 onion slice, 1 green pepper ring, 1 T. rice, ¼ C. tomatoes. Reduce heat, cover and simmer until done, about 45 minutes. Add small amount of water if necessary.

Pork Chops

4 pork chops
2 T. butter
1 onion, chopped
2 apples, peeled, cored and sliced
and/or sweet potatoes
1½ C. apple juice

Melt butter in large skillet. Brown pork chops for 2 mintues on both sides. Remove and put on plate. Saute' onions. Put pork chops and apples back into skillet and pour apple juice over them. Cover, reduce heat and simmer for 1 hour.

What Ever Casserole

1½ C. macaroni, uncooked
1 can mushroom soup
1 can tuna
1 can whole kernel corn

Drain corn into 2 C. measure and fill with milk. Combine all and cook covered 1 hour at 400°. After 20 minutes stir well. Put cover back on. About 10 minutes before it is done, cover with 1 C. grated cheese and leave cover off and cook 10-15 minutes more.

Payday Meatballs

1 can tomato soup, reserve half
1 lb. ground beef
¼ C. uncooked rice
1 egg, slightly beaten

¼ C. minced onion
2 T. minced parsley
1 tsp. salt

Shape into balls about 1½-inches in diameter. Brown in 2 T. shortening with 1 small garlic clove. Blend in rest of soup and 1 C. water. Cover and simmer about 40 minutes or utnil rice is tender, stirring now and then. Serves 4.

Cheesy Meat Loaf

1½ lbs. lean ground beef
2 C. fresh bread crumbs, 4 slices breads
1 C. tomato juice
⅓ C. chopped onion

2 eggs
2 tsp. beef flavor instant bouillon
¼ tsp. pepper
6 slices American cheese

Preheat oven to 350°. In large bowl, combine all ingredients except cheese; mix well. In shallow baking dish, shape half the mixture into loaf. Cut 4 slices cheese into strips. Arrange on meat. Top with remaining meat. Press edges together to seal. Bake 1 hour. Pour off fat. Top wiht remaining cheese slices. Refregerate leftovers.

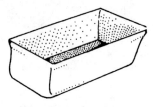

Meat Noodles

1 lb. hamburger
1 onion, chopped
1 pkg. noodles

1 can tomato soup
1 can vegetable soup
1 can water

Cook noodles. Brown hamburger and onions in skillet. Add rest of ingredients and place in a baking dish. Bake in oven for about 30 minutes or more.

Meat Loaf

1½ lbs. ground beef
¼ C. chopped onion
¾ C. oatmeal
1½ tsp. salt

½ C. catsup
¼ tsp. pepper
½ C. milk
1 beaten egg

Preheat oven to 350°. Thoroughly mix together milk, catsup, beaten egg, salt and pepper. Combine with ground beef, onion and oatmeal. Press into ungreased loaf pan and bake approximately 60-65 minutes. Drain. Let stand before slicing.

Gimmie More Meat Loaf

1½ lbs. ground beef
1 C. bread crumbs
½ tsp. salt
½ tsp. sage

1 (8 oz.) can tomato sauce
1 T. onion flakes or chopped onion
1 egg, beaten
¼ tsp. pepper

Mix and shape into loaf.

MIX AND SPREAD ON TOP:
½ C. catsup
¼ C. brown sugar

1 T. mustard
½ T. Worcestershire sauce

Bake at 350° for about 1 hour.

Rolled Meat Loaf

1½ lbs. lean ground beef
1½ tsp. salt
1/8 tsp. pepper
1 egg, slightly beaten

⅔ C. milk
2 C. bread crumbs
½ C. finely chopped onion
1 C. finely chopped celery

Mix beef with salt, pepper, egg and ½ C. of the crumbs. Add just enough milk to make mixture stick together. Mix well and place between 2 sheets of waxed paper. Flatten into a rectangle, about ½-inch thick. Combine remaining crumbs, onion, celery and ½ C. milk. Remove top waxed paper, spread stuffing on meat and roll up as for jelly roll. Place seam side down in shalow pan. Bake at 375° for about 40 minutes.

Green Pepper Steak

1 lb. beef chuck or round, fat trimmed
¼ C. soy sauce
1 clove garlic
2 stalks celery, thinly sliced
1 T. cornstarch
¼ C. salad oil

1 C. green onion, thinly sliced
1 C. red or green pepper, cut into 1-inch strips
1½ tsp. grated fresh ginger
1 C. water
2 tomatoes, cut into wedges

With a very sharp knife cut beef across grain into thin strips 1/8-inch thick. Combine soy sauce, garlic and ginger. Add beef, toss and set aside while preparing vegetables. Heat oil in large frying pan or wok. Add beef and toss over high heat until browned. Taste meat, if it is not tender, cover and simmer for 30-40 minutes over low heat. Turn heat up and toss until vegetables are tender-crisp, about 10 minutes. Mix cornstarch with water. Add. Stir and cook until thickened. Add tomatoes and heat through.

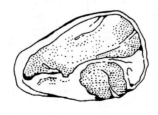

Meat Loaf

1 lb. ground beef
½ lb. ground pork
1 medium onion, finely chopped
1 clove garlic, finely chopped
½ tsp. salt
¼ tsp. crushed dried thyme
1 bay leaf, finey crushed
¼ C., fine dry bread crumbs
1 lg. egg
½ tsp. pepper

Mix all ingredients together. Rinse 7½ x 3½ x 2¼-inch loaf pan. Pack meat into loaf pan. Turn out on a small shallow baking pan. Bake 1½ hours in preheated 325° oven. (Menu: baked potato, relish plate, light dessert.)

Helen's Meat Balls

3-4 lbs. ground beef
½ tsp. salt
1 tsp. Lawry's Seasoning Salt
½ C. chopped onion

SAUCE:
2 C. catsup
2 C. brown sugar

½ C. catsup
2 eggs for every pound of meat
½ C. oatmeal for every pound of meat

¼-½ C. red wine vinegar
2-3 tsp. dry mustard

Mix as you would a meat loaf. Roll into balls. Place in 300° oven with cover over pan. Bake about 1½-2 hours, depending on size of balls. About 15 minutes before serving time, drain off excess grease. Pour sauce over the top of meat balls. Continue baking without cover for the remainder of the baking time.

Washday Meat Balls

1 lb. ground beef
½ C. homemade bread crumbs
1 T. minced onion
½ tsp. horseradish

2 drops hot pepper sauce
2 eggs, beaten
¼ tsp. salt
¼ tsp. pepper

SAUCE:
¾ C. catsup
½ C. water
¼ C. cider vinegar
3 T. brown sugar
1½ tsp. crushed onion
Cayenne pepper, to taste

2 tsp. Worcestershire sauce
½ tsp. salt
1 tsp. mustard
¼ tsp. pepper
3 drops hot pepper sauce

Heat broiler. Mix all meat ingredients and shape into balls about ½-inch to ¾-inch in size. Brown on all sides; drain fat. Combine ingredients for sauce in large Dutch oven and put meat balls into sauce. Simmer about 30 minutes or more. Makes about 3 dozen balls. (Note: Flavor improves if made a day ahead.)

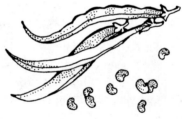

Three Bean Casserole

1 can kidney beans
1 can lima butter beans
1 can pork and beans, drained
¼ C. catsup
⅓ C. brown sugar

⅓ C. white sugar
1 sm. onion, chopped fine
1 lb. hamburger
½ lb. bacon

Fry bacon and pour off grease. Brown hamburger and onion. Mix all ingredients well. Pour in casserole and bake ½ hour at 350°.

Barbecued Brisket

4 T. beef brisket

SAUCE:
¾ C. brown sugar
½ C. catsup
Dash of nutmeg

1 tsp. mustard
1 C. barbecue sauce
Dash of Worcestershire sauce

Spinkle meat with white garlic salt, celery salt, onion salt, pepper and ½ bottle liquid smoke. Marinate overnight. Bake at 275° in covered Pyrex for 4 hours. Mix sauce ingredients together and heat. Remove meat from oven and brush with ½ of mixture. Cook ½ hour longer. Then slice and brush with rest of sauce or just put on table.

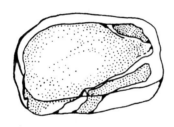

Baked Swiss Steak

1½ lbs. round steak, ¾-inch thick
¼ C. flour
1 tsp. salt
3 T. Crisco
1 (16 oz.) can stewed tomatoes

½ C. chopped celery
½ C. chopped carrot
2 T. chopped onion
½ tsp. Worcestershire sauce

Cut meat into 4 portions. Combine flour and salt; pound into meat, reserving some flour for the sauce. Brown meat in hot fat and place in shallow baking pan or dish. Blend reserved flour mixture into pan drippings in skillet. Add all other ingredients and cook, stirring constantly until mixture boils. Pour over meat. Cover and bake at 325°-350° for 2 hours or until meat and vegetables are tender.

Real Good Swiss Steak

1½-2 lbs. round steak
¼ C. flour
1 tsp. salt
Shortening

1/8 tsp. pepper
1 (10¾ oz.) can mushroom soup
1 (10½ oz.) can onion soup

Combine flour, salt and pepper. Pound into steak with a meat hammer or edge of heavy saucer. Cut into serving portions. Brown steak on both sides in hot shortening. Arrange meat in lightly greased 9 x 13 x 2-inch pan. Combine soups; pour over meat. Cover and bake in 325° oven about 1½ hours or until tender. Serve the soup mixture as gravy over potatoes, rice or noodles. Yield: 6 to 8 servings.

Beef Ribs

1 C. cider vinegar
2 T. Worcestershire sauce
1 tsp. salt
1⅓ tsp. black pepper
4 lbs. beef ribs

½ C. honey
½ C. catsup
1 tsp. dry mustard
1 clove garlic, minced

Combine all ingredients except the ribs in a saucepan. Bring to a boil, then reduce heat. Cover and simmer 15 minutes. Arrange the ribs in a single layer in baking pan. Pour hot marinade over meat. Cover and let stand for 1 hour. Drain, reserving the excess marinade. Bake the ribs at 325° for 1 hour or until tender. While cooking turn ribs frequently and baste with marinade. Serves 4.

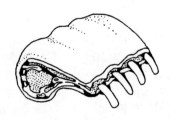

Garden Pepper Steak

1 lb. chopped steak
4 T. cooking oil
¼ C. soy sauce
Chopped tomatoes may be added during cooking for variety in taste

1½ medium green pepper
1 lg. onion
2 T. flour
1 C. cold water
Cooked rice

Brown chopped steak in oil on medium heat. Add soy sauce, cover and simmer for 15 minutes. Add flour stirred in cold water until lumps are gone. Pour over ingredients in pan, stirring as you pour. Simmer 20-30 minutes. Serve over cooked rice. Serves 4 to 6 people.

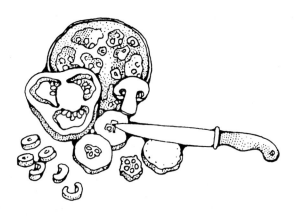

Swiss Steak

Swiss steak or thick round steak, pounded & floured - 8 oz. to person
1 pkg. dry onion soup mix

Pepper, as desired
1-2 cans beef bouillon, depending on amount of meat

Flour and brown steak. Layer in a roaster or baking pan and sprinkle with onion soup mix and pepper. Pour beef bouillon over all and bake, covered until nice and tender, 350° for 2-2½ hours. Turn meat occasionally.

Flank Steak

⅓ C. soy sauce
⅓ C. salad oil
3 T. red wine vinegar
2 tsp. chopped chutney

1 T. instant onion
1 lg. flank steak
1 /8 tsp. garlic powder

For marinade, mix together soy, oil, vinegar, chutney, garlic and onion. Pour over steak for 4 hours, turning frequently. Drain and barbeque over glowing coals, 5 minutes on each side, medium rare. Baste occasionally wiht marinade. Cut on the diagonal into thin slices to serve. To broil, allow 4 minutes on each side for rare meat. Makes 5 to 6 servings.

Salisbury Steak

1 lb. ground beef
½ lb. bulk pork sausage
1½ C cooked rice
1 tsp. salt
½ tsp. pepper

1 egg, beaten
3 C. water
1 envelope dry onion soup mix
2 T. flour

Combine beef, sausage, rice, slat, pepper and egg; mix well. Form into 6 thick steaks. Bake at 350° for 20 minutes. While the steaks are baking, combine 2½ C. of water and add onion mix and cook, covered for 10 minutes. Mix flour with remaining ½ C. of water and stir into onion soup mixture. Cook until thick. Pour over steaks and bake for 20 minutes more.

Sweet And Sour Steak

1½ lbs. cubed beef or pork
½ C. water
1 (No. 2) can pineapple chunks
1 sm. green pepper, strips
¼ C. brown sugar

2 T. cornstarch
¼ C. vinegar
3 T. soy sauce
¼ C. chopped onion
Salt, to taste

Brown meat and add water; simmer for 1 hour. Combine brown sugar, juice from pineapple, cornstarch and vinegar; mix well. Add to meat and cook until thickened. Add pineapple chunks, green peppers, onion, soy sauce and salt. Heat thoroughly. Serve over chow mein noodles.

Green Pepper Steak

1 lb. beef chuck roast or round steak, trim fat
¼ C. soy sauce
1 clove garlic
1½ tsp. grated ginger
¼ C. salad oil, peanut oil

1 C. green onion, sliced
1 C. green peppers, cut in squares
1 T. cornstarch
1 C water
2 tomatoes, cut in wedges

Cut beef across grain into thin strips 1/8-inch thick. Combine soy sauce, garlic, ginger and add beef. Toss and set aside. heat oil in wok or large skillet. Add beef and toss over high heat until browned. (If meat is not tender, cover and simmer for 30-40 minutes over low heat.) Add vegetables and toss over high heat until tender crisp. Mix cornstarch with water and add to meat and vegetables. Stir and cook until thickened. Add tomatoes and heat through. Serve over rice or noodles. Serves 4. (We have enjoyed adding cauliflower, carrots, broccoli and sugar pea pods to this basic recipe.)

Fast Meatballs

1½ lbs. ground beef
¾ C. oatmeal
½ C. milk
2 sm. onions
1½ tsp. salt

1 C ketchup
¼ C. vinegar
½ C. water
4 T. brown sugar
1 chopped onion

Combine beef, oatmeal, milk, onions and salt. Form into balls and roll in flour and brown. Put in casserole and top with ketchup, vinegar, water, sugar and onion combined. Bake at 350° for 1 hour.

Raised Meatballs

4 slices bread
½ C. milk
2 eggs
1 lb. ground beef
¾ tsp. salt
¼ tsp. pepper

2 T. chopped onion
2 tsp. baking powder
1 can cond. cream of mushroom soup
1 can cond. cream of chicken soup
1 C. milk

Soak bread in milk; add beaten eggs, ground beef, salt, pepper, onions and baking powder. Mix lightly but well; shape in balls, about size of walnuts. Brown in small amount of shortening. Place in greased baking dish. Mix the soups and milk. Pour over the meatballs and bake at 350° for 1 hour or cook in skillet, covered for 1 hour.

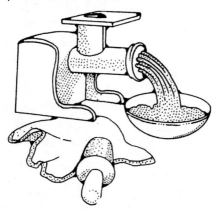

Bean Casserole

½ lb. bacon
1 lb. hamburger
1 can lima beans, drained

1 can buttered beans, drained
1 can kidney beans, drained
1 can pork and beans, drained

SAUCE:
1 T. mustard
4 T. molasses
2 T. white vinegar

½ C. brown sugar
½ C. catsup

Combine beans and meat. Mix sauce and add to other ingredients. Bake at 350° for 45 minutes.

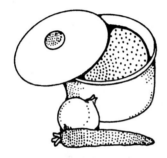

Meatballs

½ lb. hamburger
¼ C. oatmeal
½ tsp. minced onion

½ tsp. salt
Dash of pepper
½ C. milk

SAUCE:
1 T. sugar
1 T. Worcestershire sauce
½ C. ketchup

¼ C. water
1/8 C. vinegar
½ T. minced onion

Mix the first ingredients together and form small balls. Place in pan. Mix sauce and pour over balls. Bake at 350° until done.

French Toast Casserole

1 (10 oz.) long, thin loaf French or Italian bread (without seeds)
8 lg. eggs
3 C. milk
4 tsp. granulated sugar
¾ tsp. salt
1 T. vanilla extract
2 T. butter, cut into small pieces

Use extra butter to grease a 9 x 13-inch baking pan. Cut bread into 1-inch thick slices and arrange in one layer in bottom of pan. Ina large bowl, beat eggs with remaining ingredients, except butter. When thoroughly mixed, pour over bread in pan. Cover with foil and refrigerate 4-36 hours. To bake, uncover pan, dot bread with the 2 T. butter and put pan in oven. Turn oven on to 350° and bake for 45-50 minutes, until bread is puffy and lightly browned. Remove from oven and let stand for 5 minutes before serving. Makes 8 servings. Serve with a choice of syrup, honey, fresh fruit, etc.

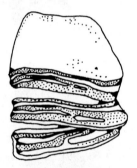

Pig Pie

2 eggs
½ C. biscuit mix
1 C. milk
½ tsp. salt
¼ C. cheddar cheese
Pepper
½ tsp. dry mustard
Cooked broccoli
3-4 strips crisped bacon
¼ C. Swiss cheese

Beat togther eggs, biscuit mix, milk, salt, pepper and mustard until smooth. Add cooked broccoli, strips of bacon and cheese. Grease 8-inch pie pan. Pour mixture into pan. Bake at 350° for 30 minutes. (You may add tomatoes, green pepper and mushrooms.)

Sausage Casserole

11 slices bread, trim crust & cube
1 lb. bulk sausage, brown & drained
9 eggs, well beaten
3 C. milk
1½ tsp. salt and pepper
1 tsp. dry mustard
8 oz. pkg. shredded cheddar cheese
½ C. chopped pepper
¼ C. chopped onion

Mix all ingredients and pour into a 9 x 13-inch pan. Bake at 350° for 1 hour or till done.

Good Time Rice And Hamburger Casserole

2 medium onions
1 lb. hamburger
1 can chicken noodle soup
1 can cream of mushroom soup
½ C. uncooked rice
1½ C. water

Brown onions and hamburger in skillet. Do not add any salt. In casserole dish combine browned onions and meat, soups, rice and water. Bake at 350° for 1 hour.

Beef And Potato Loaf

4 C. thinly sliced peeled raw potatoes
1 T. onion, cut-up

1 lb. ground beef
2/3 C. evaporated milk
1/2 C. rolled oats

1 tsp. salt
1/8 tsp. pepper
Parsley flakes (opt.)

1/4 C. catsup or chili sauce
1 tsp. salt
1/8 tsp. pepper

Arrange evenly in greased 2 quart casserole dish the sliced potatoes. Add all the above ingredients in first part. In bowl, mix the ground beef and all the ingredients in second part. Add hamburger mixture to the potatoes. Decorate top of mixture with catsup and bake 1 hour at 350° or until potatoes are done.

Ham And Egg Breakfast

8 slices bread
7 medium or 6 lg. eggs
2¾ C. milk
1 lb. ham, cubed

¾ lb. cheese, Velveeta, American cheddar, cubed
1 tsp. mustard
1 tsp. salt

Generously butter 9 x 13-inch glass baking dish. Remove crusts from bread, then cube. Layer the bread cubes, ham and cheese. Add milk to slightly beaten eggs, mustard and salt. Pour milk over layered mixture. Refrigerate overnight. Next morning bake about 1 hour at 325°.

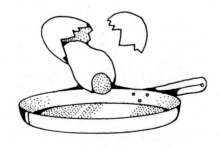

Egg-Sausage Casserole

1½ lbs. ground sausage
9 eggs
½ tsp. dry mustard
1½ C. grated cheddar cheese
3 slices bread, cubed
3 C. whole milk

Brown sausage; drain. Beat eggs slightly. Combine rest of ingredients. Place in ungreased 9 x 13-inch pan. Refrigerate overnight. Take out 1 hour before baking. Bake at 350° for 45 minutes. (If not put out ahead of time, bake at 300° for 1½ hours.)

Eggs Brunch (Make The Day Before)

4 slices bacon, sliced
½ lb. chipped beef, coarsely sliced
¼ C. butter
1 lb. fresh mushrooms, sliced and sauteed
½ C. flour
1 qt. whole milk
16 eggs
1 C. evaporated milk
¼ tsp. salt
¼ C. melted butter
Pepper

Saute' bacon and drain; remove from pan. In the same pan add chipped beef, butter and ¾ of the mushrooms. Sprinkle flour and pepper over mixture. Gradually stir in whole milk. Heat mixture, stirring until thick and smooth; set aside. Combine eggs with salt and evaporated milk and scramble in butter. In a 3 quart casserole dish, alternate layers of eggs and sauce, ending with sauce. Garnish with reserved mushrooms. Refrigerate overnight. Before serving, cover and bake 1-1½ hours at 275°.

Time To Splurge Egg Brunch

2 C. frozen hash browns, thawed
6 hard cooked eggs, whites & yolks separated, whites thinly sliced, yolks fork mashed
1 (8 oz.) can water chestnuts, thinly sliced
1 can cream of onion soup, undiluted
¼ C. sour cream
¼ C. melted butter
1 T. creamy horseradish sauce
¼ C. green pepper, diced
¼ C. green onion, chopped
2 T. butter
6 slices bacon, fried & crumbled
Pepper, to taste
½ C. shredded cheddar cheese
½ C. crushed rice cereal

Place hash browns on the bottom of a 2½ quart casserole. Top with thinly sliced egg whites and water chestnuts. Combine the cream of onion soup, sour cream, horseradish sauce and egg yolks. Saute' green pepper and onion in butter. Add to soup mixture; mix well. Pour over mixture in casserole. Sprinkle crumbled bacon on top and add pepper, to taste. Combine shredded cheese and rice cereal together and place on top of bacon. Drizzle melted butter over cereal. Bake at 375° for 30 minutes or until bubbly and brown. Garnish with parsley. Serve 4 to 6.

Barbecue Beef Sandwiches

3-4 lbs. beef roast, cooked & sliced
2½ C. ketchup
½ C. brown sugar
½ C. vinegar
1 T. horseradish
1 T. Worcestershire sauce
1 tsp. garlic salt

Mix all ingredients, except beef and bring to a boil, then simmer for about 15 minutes. Pour over beef and place in oven until beef is thoroughly warmed. Serve on buns.

BREADS

Bread

Apple Bread 97
Bread Dough 102
Cinnamon-Raised Bread 100
Farmer Dinner Rolls. 98
Hot Rolls 98
Ice Box Rolls 97
Rasin Bread 100
Spoon Rolls 99
White Bread 102, 103
Whole Wheat Bread 101, 103
Yeast Bran Bread. 99

Apple Bread

½ C. butter
1 C. sugar
2 eggs
1 tsp. vanilla
1 tsp. soda

½ tsp. salt
2 T. sour milk
2 C. diced apples
2 C. flour

TOPPING:
2 T. flour
2 T. sugar

1 tsp. cinnamon
2 T. melted butter

Cream together butter, sugar, eggs, vanilla and salt. Dissolve soda in sour milk, then add apples and flour. Add nuts, if desired. put in 2 small or 1 large greased and floured loaf pan, then mix together butter, flour, sugar ad cinnamon. Sprinkle on top of batter. Bake at 325° for 1 hour.

Ice Box Rolls

1¾ C. boiling water
1 C. light corn syrup
1 T. salt
2 tsp. shortening
1 tsp. salt

½ C. lukewarm water
2 beaten eggs
8 C. enriched white flour, sifted before measuring
2 pkgs. yeast

Mix boiling water, corn syrup, salt and shortening together. Cool to lukewarm. Soften yeast in lukewarm water and add 1 tsp. sugar. Stir into first cooled mixture. Mix in beaten eggs, stir in 4 C. flour and mix thoroughly. It is not necessary to knead. Brush top of dough with melted butter and cover tightly and store in ice box until ready to use. Shape into rolls as desired place in greased pans and let rise until doubled, in a warm place. Bake at 425° for 15-20 minutes. Two cups of whole wheat flour or graham flour may be substituted for part of the white flour. If sugar is used in place of the corn syrup, use ½ C. sugar and increase liquid to 2 cups.

Hot Rolls

2 C. hot water
2 heaping T. lard
½ C. sugar
2 beaten eggs

1½ tsp. salt
2 pkgs. dry yeast
7 C. flour
¼ C. lukewarm water

Dissolve 2 pkgs. dry yeast in ¼ C. lukewarm. Dissolve lard in hot water and cool till lukewarm. When cool, add yeast mixture and the rest of the ingredients. Then add flour to right consistency (about 7 C.). Doesn't take long to raise, about 2 hours. Make into rolls and let rise again. Bake at 400° for 10-15 minutes or until brown.

Farmer Dinner Rolls

1 C. milk
¼ C. sugar
1 tsp. salt
¼ C. margarine

½ C. warm water
2 pkgs. dry yeast
2 eggs, beaten
5¼ C. flour, unsifted

Scald milk and stir in sugar, salt and margarine. Cool to lukewarm. Measure warm water into large warm bowl. Sprinkle or crumble in yeast and stir until dissolved. Add lukewarm milk mixture, eggs and 2 C. of flour. Beat until smooth. Stir enough remaining flour to make soft dough. Turn out onto lightly floured board. Knead until smooth and elastic, about 8-10 minutes. Place in greased bowl, turning to grease top. Cover and let rise in warm place free from draft, until doubled in bulk, about 30 minutes. Punch down and turn out on lightly floured board. This dough can be made into pan rolls, crescents and cloverleaf rolls.

Spoon Rolls

1 pkg. yeast
¼ C. lukewarm water
¼ C. sugar
1 tsp. salt
⅓ C. shortening

¾ C. scalded milk
½ C. cold water
1 egg
3½ C. flour

Dissolve yeast in lukewarm water. Combine sugar, salt, shortening and scalded milk in a large bowl. Cool to lukewarm by adding ½ C. cold water. Blend in 1 egg and the dissolved yeast. Add sifted flour to mixture and mix until well blended. Place in greased bowl and cover with towel. Let rise in a warm place until double in bulk, about 45-60 minutes. Stir down dough. Spoon into well-greased muffin tins, filling ½ full. Let rise in warm place until batter has risen to edge of muffin cup and is rounded in center, about 45 minutes. Bake in medium-hot, 400° for 15-20 minutes. Makes 18 rolls.

Yeast Bran Bread

½ C. sugar
¼ C. butter
1½ tsp. salt
1 C. Bran (Kellogg's)
1 C. boiling water

2 pkgs. yeast
1 C. warm water
2 eggs, beaten
6-6½ C. flour

Combine sugar, butter, salt, Bran and boiling water. Cool. Soften yeast in warm water. Add to above mixture. Put all ingredients together and add flour; mix well. Put in greased bowl and let rise until double in bulk. Stir down and shape into 2 loaves. Let rise until double. Bake at 350° for 45 minutes.

Raisin Bread

2 pkgs. yeast
¼ C. warm water
1 C. raisins, soaked
¼ C soft margarine
¼ C. sugar

1½ tsp. salt
½ C. scalded milk or 4 T. dry milk
½ C. hot water
3¾ C. sifted flour
2 eggs, beaten

Dissolve yeast in warm water. In mixing bowl, put raisins, margarine, sugar, salt and milk. Stir until sugar is dissolved. Add yeast mixture to eggs and flour. Stir and work. Cover and let rise. Stir down when doubled in size and shape into 2 loaves. Let rise until loaf shape. Bake at 350° for 50-60 minutes.

Cinnamon-Raisin Bread

2 pkgs. dry yeast
½ C. warm water
1¾ C. warm water
3 T. sugar
1 T. salt
2 T. shortening

6-7 C. Gold Medal flour
1 C. raisins
¼ C. sugar
2 tsp. cinnamon
2 T. water
Butter, softened

Dissolve yeast in ½ C. warm water. Stir in 1¾ C. warm water, 3 T. sugar, salt, shortening and 3½ C. flour. Beat until smooth. Mix in raisins and enough remaining flour to make dough easy to handle. Turn dough onto lightly floured surface. knead until smooth and elastic, about 10 minutes. Place in greased bowl. Turn greased side up. Cover and let rise in a warm place until double, about 1 hour. (Dough is ready if an indentation remains when touched.) Punch down dough and divide into halves. Roll each half into halves. Roll each half into rectangle 18 x 9-inches. Mix ¼ C. sugar and cinnamon. Sprinkle each half with 1 T. water and half of the sugar mixture. Roll up, beginning at 9-inch side. With side of hand, press each end to seal. Fold ends under. Place seam side down in greased loaf pan. Brush with butter. Let rise until double, about 1 hour. Bake at 350° for 25-30 minutes. Remove from pans. Brush with butter and cool on rack.

Whole Wheat Bread

2 pkgs. yeast
3 C. warm water
4 C. white flour
4 T. white sugar
2 T. salt
1 C. packed brown sugar

6 T. shortening
4 C. unsifted stoneground whole
    wheat flour
2 C. pumpernickle rye flour
2 C. additional white flour

Dissolve the yeast in 3 C warm water. Add flour, sugar and salt. Let rise in a warm place until light and bubbly, about 20 minutes. Combine the brown sugar, shortening and 1 C. hot water. Let cool to lukewarm and add to risen mixture. Add whole wheat flour, pumpernickle rye flour and remaining 2 C. white flour. Mix as long as you can, then turn mixture onto table and knead for at least 15 minutes. Place in buttered bowl. Cover and let rise in warm place for 1 hour or until doubled in bulk. Turn onto a well floured table again and separate mixture into 4 balls. Cover and let stand for 15 minutes. Shape into 4 loaves. Place in greased bread pans. Let rise in pans, in warm place, covered with towel, for about 1 hour or until light. Bake at 350° for 1 hour. Remove from pans and place on racks to cool. Butter top of bread while hot and store in ice box.

Whole Wheat Bread

⅔ warm water
2 pkgs. yeast
1 tsp. brown sugar
2 T. shortening
½ C. brown sugar

1 tsp. salt
2 C. hot water
3 C. whole wheat
3 C. white flour

Mix first 3 ingredients in a small dish and let stand until bubbly, then mix the shortening, ½ C. brown sugar, 1 tsp. salt and 2 C. hot water. Stir in whole wheat flour and beat well. Mix in white flour, 1 C. at a time, beating well after each addition. It may not take all the flour. When it is stiff enough to knead, pour out on floured board, cover and let set or ''rest'' for 10-15 minutes. Knead until no longer sticky (about 10 minutes). Let rise till double, punch down and shape into 2 loaves. Let rise again and bake at 350° for 50-60 minutes.

Bread Dough

½ C. milk
½ C. sugar
1 tsp. salt
¼ C. butter

2 pkgs. yeast
½ C. water
3 eggs
4½ C. flour

Scald milk; stir in sugar, salt and butter. Dissolve yeast in warm water; add milk, eggs and half of flour. Beat well and add enough flour to make soft dough. Knead until smooth. Let rise for 1 hour. Shape into loaves or rolls; let rise. Bake at 350° until done.

White Bread

2 C. milk
5 T. sugar
1½ T. salt
5 T. lard

2 .C lukewarm water
2 pkgs. yeast
12-13 C. flour

Scald milk and add lard, sugar and salt. Cool till lukewarm. Dissolve yeast in lukewarm water and add to lukewarm milk mixture. Beat in 6 C. flour until smooth. Gradually add remaining flour (6-7 C.) until dough forms a ball and is stiff enough to be kneaded. Turn out on floured board and knead quickly and lightly until smooth and elastic. Place in greased bowl, brush with melted lard or butter, cover and let rise until doubled, in a warm place (will take 45 minutes to 1 hour). Divide dough into 4 equal portions and shape into loaves. Place in greased bread pans, cover and let rise until double in bulk, about 1 hour. Bake at 400° for about 50 minutes. Remove from pans and butter tops and sides.

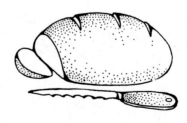

Whole Wheat Bread

6 C. milk	2 pkgs. yeast
1 C. minus 2 T. sugar	¾ C. warm water
3 T. salt	5 C. whole wheat flour
¾ C. lard	12-14 C. white flour

Scald milk and add sugar, salt and lard. Cool to lukewarm. Dissolve yeast in warm water. Add yeast to milk mixture. Add whole wheat flour and stir. Add about half of the white flour and stir. Add remaining white flour and stir. Add enough of flour to make a dough that won't stick to hands. Turn dough onto floured board or counter. Cover and let rest in warm place until doubled, about 1½ huors. Punch down and let rise again until doubled, about 1 hour. Make into 6 loaves to fit 3 of the 8½ × 4½ × 2½-inch pans and 3 of the 9½ × 5¼ × 2¾-inch pans (greased pans.) Let rise until doubled in bulk, about 1½ hours. Bake at 400° for 10 minutes. Reduce to 325° and bake for 40 minutes.

White Bread

½ C. warm water	5 T. sugar
½ tsp. sugar	1 tsp. salt
2 pkgs. yeast	2 T. lard
2 more C. warm water	5½ C. flour

Dissolve yeast in ½ C. warm water with ½ tsp. sugar. Mix 2 C. warm water with sugar, salt, melted (or soft) lard and stir in dissolved yeast. Beat in flour 2 C. at first, then add 1 C. at a time until dough is stiff enough to turn out on floured board. Let rest for 10 minutes and then knead until smooth and elastic. Put in greased bowl and cover, let rise in warm place until doubled in bulk. Shape into 3 loaves, put in greased bread pans, cover and let rise until doubled or light. Bake at 350°-375° for 30-40 minutes until nicely browned.

CAKES 'N MUFFINS 'N SUCH

CAKES 'N MUFFINS 'N SUCH

Buttermilk Muffins 113
Coffee Cake 107, 108
Cottage Cheese Muffins 112
Crazy Chocolate Cake 115
Dang Good Cake 114
Depression Cake 116
Frostless Oatmeal Cake 115
Fudge Frosting 114
Ice Box Bran Muffins 111
Oat Muffins 109
Oatmeal Muffins 110
Poverty Cake 116
Pear Bran Muffins 109
Puffs Pecan 110
Raisin Bran Muffins 113
Rhubarb Muffins 112
Yummie Bran Muffins 111
Zucchini Bread 107

One Hour Zucchini Bread

1 C. white sugar
1 C. brown sugar
3 eggs
½ C. vegetable oil
2 tsp. vanilla
3 C. flour

1 tsp. soda
½ tsp. baking powder
½ tsp. salt
2 tsp. cinnamon
2 C. zucchini, peeled and grated

Put in 3 medium loaf pans and bake at 325° for 60 minutes.

Coffee Cake

1 C. sugar
½ C. butter
1 egg
1 C. milk

2½ C. flour
2 tsp. baking powder
1 tsp. vanilla
Cinnamon-sugar mixture

Combine sugar, butter and egg. Add milk, vanilla and dry ingredients. Place half of the batter in a 8 x 8-inch pan. Cover with a cinnamon-sugar mixture. Spread remaining batter over the first layer and top with more cinnamon and sugar. Bake at 350° for 20 minutes.

Coffee Cake

1 C. butter
2 C. sugar
2 eggs
½ tsp. vanilla
1 C. sour cream
2 C. flour

1 tsp. baking soda
¼ tsp. salt
1 C. pecans
1 tsp. cinnamon
4 tsp. sugar

Cream butter and 2 C. sugar and beat in eggs, one at a time. Fold in sour cream, vanilla, flour, soda and salt. Combine the 4 tsp. sugar, cinnamon and pecans. Pour ⅓ of batter into greased bundt pan or an angel food pan. Sprinkle with ¾ pecan mixture. Add remaining batter and nut mixture. Bake at 350° for 60 minutes. Remove from pan immediately.

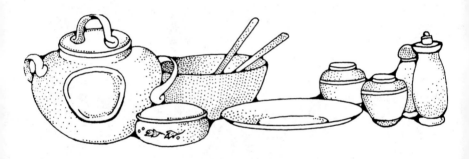

Coffee Cake

⅓ C. vegetable oil
1 egg
Milk
1 C. flour

1 C. sugar
1 tsp. baking powder
Pinch of salt

TOPPING:
⅓ C. brown sugar
1 tsp. cinnamon

Margarine, small amount

Put vegetable oil and egg in 1 C. measuring cup, fill rest of cup with milk. Put in bowl, adding dry ingredients and mix well. Spread in 8 x 8-inch pan. Sprinkle with topping and bake at 350° for 25 minutes.

Pear Bran Muffins

1 C. flour
½ C. sugar
2½ tsp. baking powder
½ tsp. salt
¼ C. whole bran cereal

1 (16 oz.) can pears in natural juice
½ C. milk
¼ C. oil
1 egg, beaten

Combine flour, sugar, baking powder and salt. Drain and dice pears; combine with bran and milk. Let stand 5 minutes. Add oil and egg to pear mixture; add all at once to flour mixture. Stir only until dry ingredients are moistened. Fill greased muffin pans ¾ full. Bake at 400° for 18-20 minutes or until wooden pick inserted near center comes out clean. Makes 1 dozen.

Oat Muffins

1 C. boiling water
¼ C. brown sugar, firmly packed
¼ C. vegetable oil
1 pkg. dry yeast
3-3½ C. flour

1 C. quick rolled oats
1 tsp. salt
1 egg
¼ C. water
Cornmeal

In a large bowl, pour boiling water over rolled oats. Stir in brown sugar, salt and oil. Cool to lukewarm. Dissolve yeast in warm water. Beat yeast and egg into oat mixture. Stir in enough flour ot make a moderately stiff dough. Cover and let rest in warm place for 30 minutes (dough does not double). Turn out on lightly floured surface and roll to ¾-inch thickness. Cut into rounds swith a 3-inch cutter. Place on greased baking sheets. Sprinkle with cornmeal. Cover and let rise in warm place until doubled, about 45 minutes. Bake on lightly greased griddle over medium heat for 20 minutes, turning every 5 minutes. Yields: 16 to 18.

Puffs Pecan

½ pt. whipping cream
1 C. chopped pecans
1 C. brown sugar
2 tubes (10 count ea.) Pillsbury biscuits

Pour whipping cream (or ¼ C. butter and ¾ milk) in a 9×13-inch pan. Mix in brown sugar and spread well. Cover with pecans. Cut in pieces or just leave whole. Put on top of nuts. Bake at 350° for 20 minutes. Let set for 15 minutes. Invert. Pull apart to serve.

Oatmeal Muffins

1½ C. sifted flour
½ C. brown sugar
2½ tsp. baking powder
¾ tsp. soda
¾ tsp. salt
¼ C. shortening
1 C. rolled oats
1 egg
1¼ C. buttermilk or sour milk

Sift together flour, sugar, baking powder, soda and salt. Cut in shortening until mixture is in coarse crumbs. Stir in oats. Add egg and buttermilk, stirring just until ingredients are moistened. Fill greased or paper cup lined muffin cups ⅔ full. Bake at 425° for 18-20 minutes.

Ice Box Bran Muffins

2 C. Bran Buds
2 C. boiling water
1 C. shortening, lard or Crisco
2 C. sugar
4 eggs

1 qt. buttermilk
5 C. flour
5 tsp. soda
1 tsp. salt
4 C. All-Bran

Let Bran Buds soak in hot water. Cream sugar and shortening. Add eggs, beating well. Sift dry ingredients. Mix buttermilk in alternately with flour. Fold in All Bran. Cover and put in ice box. These are extra nice to have on hand. Dip out as you need, but do not stir. Bake at 400°.

Yummie Bran Muffins

3 C. unprocessed bran
1 C. boiling water
2 eggs
⅓ C. corn oil
⅔ C. brown sugar

2 C. buttermilk
2½ C. whole wheat flour
1 tsp. cinnamon
2½ tsp. baking soda
½ C. raisins

Pour boiling water over bran and set aside. Beat eggs, oil and sugar together. Add buttermilk, baking soda and cinnamon; beat. Add bran and four; mix well. Add raisins. Store, covered in ice box for 12 hours. Fill Pam, greased muffin tins ⅔ full. Bake at 400° for 25 mintues. Makes 24 muffins. Mixture keeps in ice box for 6 weeks.

Cottage Cheese Muffins

1½ C. sifted flour
¼ C. sugar
4 tsp. baking powder
1 tsp. salt
1 C. sm. curd creamed cottage
⅓ C. vegetable oil
½ tsp. soda
1 C. cornmeal
1½ C. whole wheat flour
2 eggs
1 C. buttermilk

Stir together flour, sugar, baking powder, salt and soda. Stir in cornmeal and whole wheat flour. In small bowl, beat eggs. Stir in cottage cheese, buttermilk and oil. Make a well in dry ingredients. Add egg mixture stirring just enough to moisten (batter will be lumpy). Spoon into 24 greased muffin tins. Bake at 400° fro 20-30 minutes.

Rhubarb Muffins

1 C. sugar
¼ tsp. salt
3 T. margarine
2 eggs
¾ C. sour milk
1 tsp. vanilla
2½ C. flour
1 tsp. soda
1 C. raw rhubard

Mix above ingredients well. Add 1 C. chopped raw rhubarb. Bake at 375° for 20-25 minutes. Makes 18-20 muffins.

Buttermilk Muffins

1 (15 oz.) Box Raisin Bran
¾ C. sugar
5 C. flour
2 tsp. salt (opt)

5 tsp. soda
1 (4 C.)qt. buttermilk
1 C. oil
4 eggs, beaten

Mix dry ingredients; add rest. Mix thoroughly. Store in ice box in covered container. Keeps up to 6 weeks. Fill muffin tins ⅔ full. Bake at 400° for 15-20 minutes.

Raisin Bran Muffins

2 eggs
½ C. oil
1 qt. buttermilk
1½ C. sugar

2½ C. flour
1 tsp. salt
1 tsp. soda
1 lg. box Raisin Bran cereal

Mix eggs, oil, buttermilk and add sugar, flour, slat and soda. Fold in cereal. Bake in papper-lined muffin tins at 350° for 12-15 minutes. The remaining batter will keep for 4 weeks in the ice box. (Note: Let the batter sit awhile before baking the first batch.)

Dang Good Cake

1 C. brown sugar
1¾ C. water
2 tsp. cinnamon
½ C. lard

2 C. raisins
½ tsp. nutmeg
¼ tsp. cloves

Mix and boil for 3 minutes. Cool. Mix and dissolve 1 tsp. salt and 1 tsp. soda in 2 tsp. water. Add to other mixture plus 2 C. flour and 1 tsp. baking powder. Bake 50 minutes at 325°. Use greased and floured 9 x 13-inch cake pan. Eat as is or frost with powdered sugar frosting.

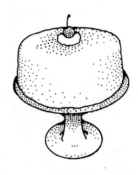

Fudge Frosting

½ C. brown sugar
½ C. white sugar
¼ C. butter

½ C. chocolate chips
½ tsp. vanilla
¼ C. milk

Put sugars, milk and butter in saucepan and bring t a boil, then turn down and add chips and vanilla. Beat until blended. Frosts 9 x 13-inch cake or 2 layers.

Frostless Oatmeal Cake

1½ C. boiling water
½ C. shortening

1 C. brown sugar
1 C. white sugar
2 eggs, beaten
1½ C. flour

1 C. oatmeal

1 tsp. baking soda
½ C. chocolate chips
1 T. cocoa

Pour first 3 ingredients together. Let stand 10 minutes. Then add the rest. Pour into pan and sprinkle on top ½ C. chocolate chips and ½ C. nuts. Bake 35-40 minutes at 350°.

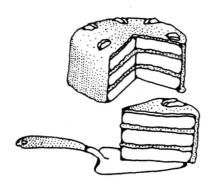

Crazy Chocolate Cake

3 C. flour
2 C sugar
6 T. cocoa
¾ C. cooking oil

2 tsp. soda
1 tsp. salt
2 T. vinegar
2 C. water

Mix all ingredients together. Put into retangle cake pan. Do not grease pan, 9 x 13-inch pan works best. Bake at 350° for 30-35 minutes.

Depression Cake

1 C. raisins
2 C. water
1 C. sugar
2 T. butter
2 C. flour

2 tsp. cinnamon
1 tsp. nutmeg
1 tsp. soda
Pinch of salt

Boil raisins and water until 1 cup of liquid is left. Cool. Combine sugar, butter and liquid from raisins. Sift together flour, nutmeg, cinnamon, soda and salt. Stir into sugar mixture. Add raisins and nuts. Place in greased and floured 9" X 12" pan. Bake at 350° for 40 to 45 minutes. Ice with brown sugar icing.

Brown Sugar Icing

2 C. powdered sugar
2 T. butter
1 tsp. maple flavor
Dash of salt
Cream (enough to make it the right consistency to spread)

Poverty Cake

2 C. brown sugar
4 T. lard
2 tsp. cinnamon
3 C. flour
1 C. raisins

2 C. hot water
2 tsp. salt
2 tsp. cloves
2 tsp. baking soda

Mix together. Bake in greased 8" X 8" pan at 350° for 40 min.

DESSERTS

DESSERTS

After Playtime Pecan Pie 128
After School Apple Crisp 133
After School Apple Pie 131
After The movie Lemon Pie 123
Ann's Pie Crust 125
Apple Cake 152
Apple Crisp 134, 147, 156
Apple Dessert 153
Back Pasture Gooseberry Pie 125
Baked Custard 128
Banana Split 142
Blueberry Dessert 139
Blue Ribbon Pie 122
Bread Pudding 137
Butterscotch Sauce Ice Cream Topping 133
Can't Wait Cherry Cobbler 154
Cheesecake 140
Cherry Dessert 146,148,151
Cherry Pie 123, 126
Chocolate Cherry Creams 153
Chocolate Sauce 145
Clara's Rhubarb Torte 145
Coconut Pie 126
Coconut Pudding 136
Date Pudding 135
Fruit Cobbler 151
Fruit Shortcake 141
Good Hot Apple Dumplings 134
Good To The Last Crumb German Cheese Cake 141
Great Pie Crust 129
Hot Chocolate Syrup 145
Hot Fudge Sauce 132
Iowa Pie Crust 130
Jello Pudding Roll 144
Lemon Cheesecake 138
Lemon Pudding 136
Luscious Cherry Cake 147

- 118 -

DESSERTS-CONTINUED

Mama's Oatmeal Pie 122
Marshmallow Dessert 143
Meringue 121
Milkin' Time Butterscotch Pie 124
Mom's Fruit Cobbler 156
More Apple Cake 129
My First Apple Crisp Pudding 135
Oatmeal 'N Apple Pudding 150
October Apple Crisp 150
Old Fashioned & Real Cheap Bread Pudding 143
Orange Pudding 141
Oreo Dessert 153
Party Time Pineapple-Coconut Torte 152
Peach Upside Down Cake 146
Peanut Butter Pie 130
Pecan Pie 131
Penny Saved Tapioca Pudding 136
Peppermint Chiffon Pie 127
Pie Crust With Milk 124
Rena's Coconut Pie 125
Real Cheap Cocoa Pudding 142
Real Good Rhubarb Dessert 148
Rhubarb Crisp 149
Rhubarb Dessert 149
Rhubarb Pie 121, 127
Special Cake Squares 155
Special Treat Ice Cream Toppings 132
Spice Cake 155
Strawberry Graham Cracker Dessert 154
Super Pie 126
Sweet Tooth Vanilla Wafer Dessert 144
Tapioca Pudding 137
Velma's Apple Pie 131
Wanda's Crisp 138
Y'All Come Dessert 140
Yummie Strawberry Squares 139

Rhubarb Pie

2 eggs, slightly beaten
1 C. sugar
⅓ C flour
½ tsp. baking powder

1 C. milk
½ stick melted butter
2 C. diced rhubarb

(Forms its own crust.) Bake at 350° for 40 minutes. (I sometimes double the recipe and bake in a 9×13-inch pan.)

Meringue

1 T. cornstarch
2 T. cold water
½ C. boiling water
3 egg whites

6 T. sugar
1 tsp. vanilla
Pinch of salt

Blend cornstarch and cold water in saucepan. Add boiling water and cook, stirring until thick and clear. Let stand until cold. Beat egg whites until foamy. Gradually add sugar and beat until stiff, but not dry, on low speed. Add salt and vanilla. Gradually beat in cold cornstarch mixture. Turn on high speed and beat well. Spread over cooled pie filling. Bake at 350° for 10 minutes. This meringue cuts perfectly and never gets sticky.

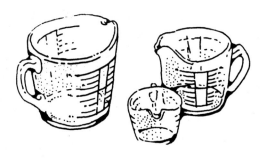

Mama's Oatmeal Pie

3 eggs, beaten
⅔ C. white sugar
1 C. brown sugar
2 T. butter
⅔ C. coconut
⅔ C. oatmeal
1 tsp. vanilla
¼ C. nutmeats, pecans preferred
Unbaked pie shell

Beat eggs, sugar, butter and vanilla together. Add coconut and oatmeal. Put in unbaked pie shell. Sprinkle with nutmeats. Bake at 350° for 35 minutes.

Blue Ribbon Pie

1 (14 oz.) can sweetened cond. milk
½ C. brown sugar
½ C. pecans, chopped
¼ tsp. burnt sugar flavoring
1 baked pie shell
1 C. coconut

Combine milk and brown sugar in top of double boiler. Cook over boiling water until thick. Add pecans, flavoring and coconut. Put in baked pie shell and chill. Top pie with whipped cream and garnish with pecan halves. Chill until time to serve. Very rich!

After The Movie Lemon Pie

4 egg yolks, beaten
1¾ C. sugar
5 T. cornstarch
1 T. butter
2 C. water
Juice of 2 medium-sized lemons

Mix ingredients and cook until thickened. Pour in baked pie shell. Use egg whites to make your favorite meringue.

Cherry Pie

1 can drained cherries
1 T. flour
1 C. sugar
¼ C. butter
2 egg yolks
¼ C cream
½ tsp. vanilla

Put cherries in unbaked pie crust. Cream the butter, flour and sugar. Add egg yolks, beat until smooth. Add cream and vanilla. Pour this mixture over cherries. Place in hot oven, 450° for 10 minutes. Reduce heat to 355° and bake for 30 minutes. Make meringue from egg whites and 2 T. sugar. Put on top of berry mixture and brown.

Milkin' Time Butterscotch Pie

1 C. brown sugar
2 T. flour
1 C. cold milk
2 beaten egg yolks

2 T. butter
1 tsp. vanilla
Pinch of salt

Combine all ingredients in the order given. Place over heat and stir constantly until mixture thickens and is thoroughly cooked. Pour in baked pie crust and cover with meringue made of the two egg whites

Pie Crust With Milk

1 C. flour
½ tsp. salt

¼ C. shortening or lard
2⅓ T. (about) cold milk

Makes one 8-inch or 9-inch crust.

Ann's Pie Crust

3 C. flour
1 tsp. salt
1 C. shortening

1 egg, beaten
1/3 C. water
1 tsp. vinegar

Blend flour, salt and shortening together. Stir in egg and liquid; roll. Can be rerolled without getting tough. Makes three 9-inch pie shells.

Back Pasture Gooseberry Pie

4 C. green gooseberries
3/4-1 C. sugar, depending on sourness of berries

1½ T. flour
1/8 tsp. salt
1½ T. butter

Combine sugar, flour and salt. Sprinkle over berries, stirring to distribute. Turn into pie shell, dot with butter and brush edge of pastry with water. Cover with pastry and slash. Bake in 450° oven for 15 minutes or until crust is delicately browned. Reduce heat to 350° and continue baking for 20-25 minutes or until berries are tender.

Rena's Coconut Pie

1 (9-inch) pie crust, unbaked
4 eggs or 8 egg yolks
2/3 C. sugar

½ tsp. salt
2/3 C. milk or cream
1½ C. fresh toasted coconut

Mix eggs, sugar, salt and milk. Add 1 C. coconut and pour into crust. Bake on lowest oven rack at 400° for 15 minutes. Turn heat down to 350° and bake for 25-30 minutes. The last 5-10 minutes, add the rest of the coconut.

Super Pie

1 scant C. sugar
½ C. flour
2 C. milk
1 C. coconut

1 tsp. vanilla
¼ lb. butter
4 eggs

Mix well. Pour into a 9-inch buttered pie plate and bake at 350° for 40-50 minutes or until done.

Coconut Pie

1 (9-inch) unbaked pie crust
3 eggs
1 T. flour
¾ C. sugar

1 C. light corn syrup
2 T. butter, melted
1 tsp. vanilla
1½ C. coconut

Beat eggs, sugar and flour. Add syrup and melted butter and beat. Add vanilla and beat. Sprinkle coconut over bottom of unbaked pie crust. Pour the mixture over the coconut. Bake in slow 325° oven for 40-45 minutes or until firm.

Cherry Pie

2 (1 lb. ea.) cans water-packed red tart cherries
3 T. cornstarch

2 T. liquid sugar substitute
½ tsp. almond extract
1 (9-inch) baked pie shell

Drain cherries and pour juice into blender container. Add cornstarch and sugar substitute and blend for 20 seconds. Pour into saucepan, cook and stir over medium heat until thick, about 5 minutes. Cool to room temperature, add drained cherries and flavoring. Pour into baked pie shell. Makes 6 servings.

Peppermint Chiffon Pie

14 chocolate sandwich cookies
3 T. butter
1 env. unflavored gelatin
¾ C. finely crushed peppermint hard candy
1 C. milk
4 egg whites
2 T. sugar
1 C. heavy cream, whipped

Crush cookies in plastic bag wiht rolling pin (make about 1¼ C.). If fillings stick to inside of bag, scrape off the rubber spatula and blend with crumbs Melt butter in medium-sized skillet; stir in cookie crumbs, remove from heat, and stir for 1 minute. Press crumb mixture against sides and bottom of 9-inch pie plate. Chill while preparing filling. Sprinkle gelatin over milk in small heavy saucepan; let stand a few minutes to soften. Add ½ C. of crushed candy. Cook, stirring constantly, over medium heat until gelatin is completely dissolved. Place pan in bowl of ice and water to speed setting; chills, stirring often, until mixture starts to thicken. While gelatin mixture chills, beat egg whites in medium-size bowl until foamy white; gradually beat in sugar until meringue stands in soft peaks. Fold whipped cream, 2 T. reserved crushed candy and meringue into gelatin mixture until no streaks of white remain; spoon into chilled pie crust. Chill for 4 hours or until firm.

Vinegar Pie

1 C. sugar
3 eggs, beaten until thick
1/3 C. apple cider vinegar
1/2 tsp. lemon extract
2 T. flour
1 C. water
small lump of butter

Combine sugar, eggs, vinegar, flour and water in double boiler and cook until thick and smooth. Stirring occasionally. Just before removing from heat, stir in butter and lemon extract. Pour into baked pie shell.

After Playtime Pecan Pie

¼ C. butter
¾ C. sugar
1 tsp. vanilla
2 T. flour
3 eggs

½ C. Kahlua
½ C. dark corn syrup
¾ C. evaporated milk
1 C. pecans
Pie shell

Cream butter, sugar, vanilla and flour. Add eggs, 1 at a time. Stir in remaining ingredients. Pour into unbaked pie shell. Bake at 400° for 10 minutes. Turn oven down to 325° and bake for 40 minutes more or until set. Makes 1 deep dish pie.

Baked Custard

6 eggs
¾ C. sugar
½ tsp. salt

4 C. scalded milk
½ tsp. vanilla
Nutmeg, as desired

Beat eggs; add sugar and salt; mixing well. Add milk, scalded or not and vanilla. Bake at 350°-375° for 1-1½ hours, depending on depth of baking dish. Place baking dish in larger pan that has 1-1½-inch of hot water in it, to bake.

More Apple Cake

4 C. diced apples
1½ C. white sugar
½ C. oil
1 C. chopped nuts
2 tsp. vanilla

2 C. unsifted flour
2 tsp. soda
1 tsp. cinnamon
½ tsp. salt

ICING:
½ C. canned milk
¼ lb. stick butter

1 C. white sugar

Mix apples and sugars together. Let stand while making the following. Mix the oil, chopped nuts, vanilla; add unsifted flour, soda, cinnamon and salt. Combine all ingredients. Bake at 350° for 50 minutes or until it leaves the side of the pan. (Grease pan.) Makes a large cake. (I use Pyrex baking pan or roasting pan.) For icing: (Icing ingredients can be cut in half.) mix the canned milk, sugar and butter in a saucepan. Bring to a boil. Pour over cake while hot.

Great Pie Crust

3 C. flour
1¼ C. shortening
¼ tsp. salt

1 tsp. vinegar
1 egg
6 T. water

Blend flour, salt and shortening until about the size of peas. Add remaining ingredients and mix well. Add more water, if necessary, a teaspoon at a time. Divide in half and roll out to desired thickness. Makes two 9-inch crusts.

Peanut Butter Pie

1 baked 9-inch pie shell

BOTTOM:
1 C. powdered sugar   ⅓ C. creamy peanut butter

FILLING:
¼ C. cornstarch   2 C. scalded milk
⅔ C. sugar   3 egg yolks, beaten
¼ tsp. salt   ¼ tsp. vanilla

TOPPING:
3 egg whites, beaten

For bottom layer, mix powdered sugar and peanut butter until like cornmeal. Spread ½ of this mixture in bottom of baked pie shell. For filling, combine cornstarch, sugar, salt, scalded milk and beaten egg yolks. Cook until thick. Add vanilla and spread over peanut butter layer in pie crust. For topping, beat egg white. Spread over pie filling and sprinkle with rest of peanut butter mixture over egg whites. Bake until light brown, 20 minutes.

Iowa Pie Crust

3 C. flour   1 egg, slightly beaten
1 tsp. salt   ½ tsp. vinegar
1 C. lard   5 T. ice water

Cut lard into flour and salt until particles are the size of peas. Mix in the egg, vinegar and ice water. Gather pastry into a bowl and roll out on floured pastry sheet. Makes 2 double crust pies.

After School Apple Pie

1 egg
¾ C. sugar
1 tsp. vanilla
½-¾ C. flour
2 tsp. baking powder
1 C. chopped apples and nuts

Beat egg and sugar; add vanilla, flour and baking powder. Mix together and add chopped apples and nuts. Put in greased round cake pan. Bake at 350° for 25 minutes.

Velma's Apple Pie

6 C. sliced tart juicy apples
¾ C. sugar
¾ tsp. cinnamon
1 T. butter

Preheat oven to 425°. Combine apples, sugar and spice. Heap into pastry lined pie pan; dot with butter. Cover with top crust. Seal and flute edges. Bake at 425° for 50-60 minutes or until done.

Pecan Pie

3 eggs
1 C. light corn syrup
½ C. sugar
1 T. butter, melted
1 tsp. vanilla
1⅓ C. pecan halves
Pie shell

Beat eggs lightly. Add syrup, sugar, butter, vanilla and pecans. Pour into 9-inch unbaked pie shell. Bake at 375° for 40-50 minutes.

Special Treat Ice Cream Toppings

HONEY-NUT:
¾ C. honey   ⅓ C. chopped walnuts or pecans

Mix all together. Makes about 1 C. of topping.

HONEY-BERRY:
¾ C. honey   ¾ C. strawberry jam or preserves

Mix all together. Makes 1½ C. of topping.

Hot Fudge Sauce

1 C. sugar   1 C. water
2 heaping T. cornstarch   1 T. butter
¼ C. cocoa   ½ tsp. vanilla

Mix first 3 ingredients well with spoon. Add water and butter and cook mixture until thick. Watch carefully and stir occasionally at beginning and continually near end. When thick, remove from heat and stir in vanilla. Serve over ice cream. Delicious!

Butterscotch Sauce Ice Cream Topping

1 C. white corn syrup
1 C. white sugar
Pinch of salt (¼ tsp.)
1 C. brown sugar

1 C. water
½ tsp. vanilla
½ C. cream or 1 sm. can evaporated milk

Mix corn syrup, white and brown sugar with 1 C. water. Simmer for 10 minutes. Cool to lukewarm. Stir in ½ C. cram or 1 small can evaporated milk and add salt and vanilla. Serve hot or cold over ice cream. If you have some left put in a jar and store in ice box.

Bread Pudding

2¼ C. milk
2 slightly beaten eggs
2 C. (1-inch) day old bread cubes
½ C. brown sugar

½ tsp. cinnamon
1 tsp. vanilla
¼ tsp. salt
½ C. seedless raisins (opt.)

Combine milk and eggs, pour over bread cubes. Stir in remaining ingredients. Bake at 350° about 45 minutes or until a knife comes out clean. Top with whipped cream or ice cream.

After School Apple Crisp

6 apples, sliced
1 C. sugar
1 T. cinnamon

2 C. brown sugar
1 C. flour
¼ C. butter

Mix apples, sugar and cinnamon; put in bottom of pie pan. Mix brown sugar, flour and butter. Put on top. Bake at 350° for 30-35 minutes. Let cool and serve with whipped cream.

Good Hot Apple Dumplings

SYRUP:
2 C. sugar
2 C. water
¼ tsp. cinnamon

¼ tsp. nutmeg
¼ C. butter

DOUGH:
2 C. flour
1 tsp. salt
2 tsp. baking powder

¾ C. shortening
½ C. milk

Make syrup of sugar, water, cinnamon and nutmeg; add buter. Pare and core apples, cut into fourths. Sift flour, salt and baking powder. Cut in shortening. Add milk all at once and stir until moistened. Roll ¼-inch thick, cut into 5-inch squares. Arrange 4 pieces of apple on each square, sprinkle generously with additional sugar, cinnamon and nutmeg, dot with butter. Fold corners to center, pinch edges together. Place 1-inch apart in greased baking pan about 9 x 13-inch pan. Pour syrup over them. Bake in moderate oven, 375°, about 35 minutes. Makes 8 dumplings.

Apple Crisp

1¼ C. oatmeal
1¼ C. flour
1 C. brown sugar

⅔ C. shortening
4 C. apples

1½ C. white sugar
4 T. cornstarch

1½ C. water

Mix dry ingredients together. Add the shortening and blend well. Pat ⅔ of mixture in bottom of 9 x 13-inch pan. Spread with cut-up apples. Cook whtie sugar, cornstarch and water until clear. Pour over apples. Sprinkle remaining crumb mixture. Bake at 350° for 1 hour. Let stand for 15 minutes after oven is turned off. Serve warm or cold with whipped cream.

Date Pudding

1½ C. sugar
2 eggs, beaten
1¼ tsp. soda
1 C. boiling water

1½ T. shortening
1½ C. flour
1 C. nuts
1 C. chopped dates

FILLING:
½ lb. chopped dates
⅔ C. water

½ C nuts

Whipped cream

Cream shortening and sugar until fluffy. Add beaten eggs and beat well. Sift flour and soda; blend with creamed mixture. Add nuts, dates and boiling water. Pour into a greased and floured 11 x 9 x 2-inch pan. Bake at 350° for 35 minutes. For filling: Cook dates and water until thick. Stir in nuts and spread on cake. Serve with whipped cream.

My First Apple Crisp Pudding

6-8 apples, sliced
1 tsp. cinnamon
½ C. water

½ C. butter
1 C. sugar
¾ C. flour

Butter casserole and add apples, water and cinnamon. Work together sugar, flour and butter until crumbly; sprinkle over apple mixture. Bake, uncovered at 350° for 30 minutes.

Coconut Pudding

CRUNCH:
1 C flour
¼ C. brown sugar

½ C. soft butter
1 C. coconut

1 pkg. vanilla pudding mix
2 C. milk
Pinch of salt
3 eggs, separated

2 T. butter
1 tsp. vanilla
½ tsp. banana flavoring
2-3 bananas

For crunch: Mix flour and brown sugar, cut in butter and mix until crumbly. Add coconut and mix until blended. Mix pudding mix, salt, milk and egg yolks. Cook as directed on package. Add butter, vanilla and banana flavoring. Beat egg whites with ¼ C. sugar and fold into cooked pudding. Layer into the pan, first crunch, then pudding, bananas, pudding, bananas, and end with crunch.

Penny Saved Tapioca Pudding

3 eggs, separated
1 C. sugar
1 qt. milk

¼ heaping C. tapioca
1 tsp. vanilla

Mix and boil 3 egg yolks; beaten, sugar, milk and tapioca. Beat egg whites stiff and add to mixture. Remove from heat and add vanilla; stir well.

Lemon Pudding

1 C. sugar
1 T. butter
1 lemon, juice & rind

2 T. flour
2 eggs
1 C. milk

Cream 1 C. sugar with 1 T. butter. Add juice and rind of 1 lemon, 2 T. flour, yolks of 2 eggs, 1 C. milk and last add beaten whites of 2 eggs. Set in a pan of warm water until done, or for about 1 hour (350°).

Bread Pudding

¾ C. (or less) brown sugar
3 slices bread, cubed
3 eggs, beaten
1½ C. milk

½ tsp. vanilla
½ tsp. cinnamon
½ C raisins

Put brown sugar in bottom of greased double boiler. Add bread cubes. Don't stir. Add raisins. Beat eggs with milk and pour over mixture. Do not stir or peek. Cook for 1 hour with lid on. Keep water boiling.

Tapioca Pudding

3 eggs, separated
1 C sugar
1 qt. milk

¼ heaping C. tapioca
1 tsp. vanilla

Mix and boil 3 egg yolks; beaten, sugar, milk and tapioca. Beat egg whites stiff and add to mixture. Remove from heat and add vanilla; stir well.

Lemon Cheesecake

1 (8 oz.) pkg. cream cheese
½ C. milk
1½ C. milk
1 sm. pkg. instant lemon pudding mix

17 graham cracker halves
¼ C. melted butter
Graham cracker crumbs or cherry or blueberry pie filling

Stir cream cheese till very soft. Gradually blend in ½ C. milk till smooth. Add 1½ C. milk and lemon pudding mix. Beat slowly with egg beater for 1 minute. Pour at once into graham cracker halves and melted butter. Top with graham cracker crumbs or the cherry or blueberry pie filling.

Wanda's Crisp

3-4 medium sized apples
½ tsp. cinnamon
½ C. brown sugar
½ C. oatmeal

½ C. sugar
½ C. butter or margarine
½ C. flour

Slice apples into 8 x 8-inch butter pan. Sprinkle with sugar and cinnamon. Place over low heat and partially cook while mixing topping. Mix remaining ingredients together and spread over apples. Bake at 350° for about 25 minutes or until browned. This is easy to remember, because everything is measured by halves.

Blueberry Dessert

22 graham crackers
½ C. melted butter
¼ C. sugar

2 cans blueberry pie mix
2 C. whipping cream
1 (10 oz.) pkg. miniature marshmallows

Mix well the graham crackers, melted butter and sugar for crust. Put half of crust in bottom of pan. Whip cream and add marshmallows. Place half on top of crust. Add blueberry pie mix to next layer, whipped cream to next layer and top with remaining graham crackers.

Yummie Strawberry Squares

2 (3 oz. ea.) pkgs. strawberry gelatin
20 oz. pkg. strawberries
1 (3 oz.) pkg. cream cheese

3 C. boiling water
1 C. boiling water
1 (8 oz.) can crushed pineapple
1 container whipped cream

Dissolve strawberry gelatin in 3 C. boiling water. Immediately add strawberries, stirring until completely thawed. Pour into lightly oiled 13 x 9-inch pan. Chill until partially set. Meanwhile, drain pineapple, reserving juice. Dissolve lemon gelatin in 1 C. boiling water. Stir in reserved juice. Place cream cheese in blender jar. Add hot lemon gelatin until smooth. Stir in pineapple. Chill until thick and syrupy. Fold in whipped cream. Spread over gelatin in pan and chill until set. Makes 12 servings.

Y'All Come Dessert

12 graham crackers, 1⅓ C. crushed
2 T. sugar
¼ C butter
Juice & grated rind of 1 lemon

1 C. whipping cream
½ C. sugar
3 eggs, separated

For crumb crust, mix graham crackers, 2 T. sugar and butter. Put in refrigerator to set and chill while mixing filling. For filling, beat egg yolks. Add lemon and sugar, beaten egg whites and fold in whipped cream. Put in graham cracker crust. Save a few crumbs to sprinkle on top. Freeze. You can use a pie pan or a square pan.

Cheesecake

1 (3 oz.) pkg. lemon Jello
1 (8 oz.) pkg. cream cheese
1 (13 oz) can evaporated milk
1 C. sugar
1 tsp. vanilla

28 graham cracker squares
1 T. powdered sugar
1 stick butter
½ C. nuts

Combine graham cracker crumbs, rolled fine with the powdered sugar and butter. Save some crumbs for the topping. Pat into 9 x 13-inch pan and bake at 350° for 5-8 minutes. Mix lemon Jello with 1 C. boiling water. Cool until slightly jelled. Beat together cream cheese, sugar and vanilla. Add cooled Jello. Beat evaporated milk until consistency of whipped cream. Mix into cream cheese with spatula. Pour over crust and top with graham crackers and nuts.

Good To The Last Crumb German Cheese Cake

4 C. pot cheese
4 eggs
1 C. sugar
¼ C. melted butter

1 C. light cream or Rich milk
1 T. cornstarch
1 T. vanilla
1 tsp. salt

Put cheese through a strainer and beat eggs until light. Then combine all ingredients. Use rich biscuit dough for bottom crust. Fill with mixtures and sprinkle with cinnamon. Bake at 450° for 15 minutes and then at 375° for 1 hour.

Fruit Shortcake

2 C. sifted flour
3 tsp. baking powder
1 tsp. salt
¼ C. sugar

⅓ C. Crisco or lard
1 egg, beaten
⅔ C. milk

Mix all dry ingredients. Cut in shortening until mixture looks like coarse meal. Add milk and egg, stirring just enough to hold dough together. Place dough on board which has been dusted with flour. Knead lightly several times and roll dough about ¾-inch thick. Cut with floured cutter or just pat dough out in pie plate or round cake pan. Sprinkle a little sugar on top of shortcake. Bake in hot oven, 425° for 15-20 minutes or until brown as desired.

Orange Pudding

3 eggs
2 tsp. flour
1 C. sugar
1¼ C. water

1 tsp. lemon juice
3 oranges, cut fine
2 T. sugar

Beat egg yolks until fluffy. Sift in flour and sugar. Add water and boil until it thickens. Add lemon juice. Pour over cut-up oranges. Add beaten whites of eggs, sweetened with 2 T. sugar.

Real Cheap Cocoa Pudding

1 C. sugar
4 T. flour, rounded
4 T. cocoa, level
½ tsp. salt

2½ C. boiling water
Butter, size of walnut
2 tsp. vanilla

Mix flour, cocoa, sugar and salt; add boiling water slowly and stir well. Cook until thick. Add vanilla and butter.

Banana Split

3 C. crushed graham crackers
½ butter
2 C. sugar
2 eggs
1 tsp. vanilla
Bananas
Nuts

Miniature chocolate chips
1 can crushed pineapple, drained
1 lg. container Cool Whip
Maraschino cherries, drained and halved
Sliced strawberries

Melt ½ of butter and combine with graham crackers. Pat into 11 x 13-inch pan. Mix other half of butter, sugar, eggs and vanilla with electric mixer for 10 minutes. Spread over graham cracker crust. Sprinkle with chips. Layer pineapple, bananas and strawberries. Cover with whipped cream. Top with chopped pecans and cherries. Refrigerate overnight for easier cutting and serving.

Old Fashioned & Real Cheap Bread Pudding

8 slices of bread, broken up	3 eggs
1 C. sugar	1 qt. milk
1 C. raisins	1 tsp. salt

Combine all ingredients and put in cake pan. Bake at 350° for 45 minutes or knife inserted 1-inch from edge comes out clean.

Marshmallow Dessert

30 lg. marshmallows	½ pt. cream
½-¾ C. pineapple	14 graham crackers, crushed fine
1 C. milk	

Dissolve marshmallows in milk in a double boiler; set aside to cool. Whip the cream. Roll cracker crumbs fine and put half in bottom of 9 x 13-inch pan. Drain pineapple and add to marshmallows and milk. Fold in whipped cream. Spoon the mixture on the crumbs and sprinkle balance of crumbs on top. Place in ice box for about 8 hours so as to serve cold.

Sweet Tooth Vanilla Wafer Dessert

2 C. crushed vanilla wafers
¼ lb. butter, melted
2 eggs
2 sticks oleo
3½ C. powdered sugar
1 tsp. vanilla

5 medium bananas
1 lg. can crushed pineapple
Cool Whip
Chopped pecans
Maraschino cherries

Mix together wafers, melted butter and press into pan. Beat for 5 minutes the 2 eggs, 2 sticks oleo, powdered sugar and vanilla. Spread over vanilla wafers. Slice and spread 5 medium bananas over above ingredients. Spread large can of crushed pineapple, drained over all. Top with a large container of whipped cream. Garnish with chopped pecans and maraschino cherries. Refrigerate overnight.

Jello Pudding Roll

3 eggs
1 C. sugar
¼ C. cold water
1 tsp. vanilla
1 C. sifted all-purpose flour

2 tsp. baking powder
½ tsp. salt
1 pkg. lemon Jello pudding
½ C. sugar
1 egg

Beat eggs until thick and lemon colored, 5 minutes. Add sugar gradually, continuing to beat until light and fluffy. Add water and vanilla. Add sifted dry ingredients and blend until smooth. Pour into greasd wax paper lined 15-inch jelly roll pan. Bake at 375° for 12-15 minutes. Turn out immediately onto tea towel, sprinkle with powdered sugar. Remove waxed paper. Trim any rough edges and roll cake up in cloth and place on rack to cool. Mix contenst of Jello package and ½ C. sugar, substitute 1 whole egg for 2 yolks as indicted on package. Prepare as directed; cool. Unroll cake and spread on cooled filling. Roll up again and chill until ready to serve.

Chocolate Sauce

1 C. sugar
¼ C. milk
1 T. cocoa
¼ C. butter

In saucepan combine all of the above listed ingredients. Then cook over low heat and stir until sugar dissolves. Serve over ice cream or fruit.

Hot Chocolate Syrup

1 C. sugar
⅓ C. cocoa
1 T. butter
2 T. corn syrup
½ tsp. vanilla
1/8 tsp. salt

Melt butter in pan; add cocoa and stir over low heat until melted. Add boiling water gradually. Add sugar and syrup. Cook for 5 minutes, stirring often. Add vanilla and salt. Very good on ice cream.

Clara's Rhubarb Torte

3 C. diced rhubarb
1 C. sifted flour
1 C. sugar
¾ T. salt
1 unbeaten egg
½ C. shortening
1 tsp. baking powder

Place rhubarb in square pan. Put ½ C. sugar over rhubarb. Mix flour, ½ C. sugar, salt, egg, shortening and baking powder; sprinkle over rhubarb. Bake in moderate oven.

Peach Upside Down Cake

1 C. brown sugar
½ C. Crisco
1 C. white sugar
½ C. Crisco
1 egg
½ C. milk

1½ C. flour
2 tsp. baking powder
¼ tsp. salt
1 tsp. vanilla
Peaches

Place brown sugar and Crisco in large iron skillet. When melted, place in pan as many sliced or halved peaches as possible. Pour the cake mixture over peaches. Bake at 350° for 40 minutes. Turn out on cake plate, peach side up. May be served with whipped cream.

Cherry Dessert

2 C. vanilla wafers, crushed
¼ C. butter, melted
1½ C. powdered sugar
8 oz. pkg. Phil. cream cheese

½ pt. cream, whipped
1 can cherry pie filling
½ C. sugar
2 T. cherry Jello mix

Combine vanilla wafers and butter. Press into botom of square pan for crust. Mix well the powdered sugar and cream cheese. Add the cream and pour over crust. Heat cherry pie filling with sugar and cherry Jello. When cool, pour over second layer and chill.

Luscious Cherry Cake

¼ C. melted shortening
¾ C. sugar
2 eggs, separated
½ C. milk
1½ C. flour

3 tsp. baking powder
¼ tsp. salt
1 tsp. vanilla
2 C. cherries, drained

SAUCE:
1 C. cherry juice
¼ C. water
1½ T. cornstarch

1 C. cherries
¼ C. sugar, or more
1 T. butter

Mix sugar, shortening and egg yolks. Stir in dry ingredients, sifted together, alternately with the milk and vanilla. Fold in cherries and beaten egg whites. Bake at 350° for 35-40 minutes. Serve squares of cake with the sauce which is made by heating the cherry juice and sugar to boiling and then adding the 1½ T. cornstarch that has been moistened with the ¼ C. water. Cook until slightly thickened and add cherries and butter. If cherries are real sour, you may want more sugar.

Apple Crisp

8-10 apples
½ C. water

½ tsp. cinnamon

TOPPING:
½ C. brown sugar
½ C. white sugar

¾ C. flour
½ C. butter

Place apples in a greased 8×8-inch pan. Sprinkle water and cinnamon over apples. Mix other ingredients together until crumbly. Pour over the top of apples. Bake 35-40 minutes at 350°.

Real Good Rhubarb Dessert

Rhubarb
1½ C. sugar
2 (3 oz. ea.) boxes Jello, strawberry raspberry or cherry
1½ C. flour
½ C. powdered sugar
¾ C. butter

In a 9×13-inch pan, cut-up rhubarb to fill the pan ¾ full. Mix the sugar and Jello together and mix in the rhubarb well. Mix the flour, powdered sugar and butter utnil crumbly, then sprinkle on top of the rhubarb mixture, evenly. Bake at 350° for 30 minutes. Serve with whipped cream.

Cherry Dessert

1¼ C. flour
½ C. sugar
⅔ C. butter
½ C. nuts (opt.)
1 (8 oz.) pkg. cream cheese
1 C. powdered sugar
1 C. whipped topping
5 C. pitted cherries, can use home grown
3 T. tapioca
3 T. cornstarch
1¼ C. sugar
1 tub whipped topping

Mix flour, sugar, butter and nuts together and pat in bottom of 9×13-inch pan and bake 15 minutes. Brown very slightly in 350° oven. Mix cream cheese, sugar and topping together well and spread over cooled crust. Mix cherries and tapioca together and let set 10 minutes. Then put on medium heat, when it starts to bubble; add the cornstarch and sugar. Simmer and stir until nice and thick. Cool well before putting over the cream cheese layer. Cover cherry mixture with a whipped topping. Keep in ice box.

Rhubarb Dessert

1½ C. flour
7 T. powdered sugar
¾ C. butter
2½ C. sugar
¼ C. flour

1 tsp. vanilla
3 beaten eggs
Dash of salt
1 C. evaporated milk

Crumb flour, powdered sugar and butter; pat in ungreased 9 x 13-inch pan. Bake at 325° for 15 minutes. Sprinkle 4 C. or more rhubarb on hot crust. Then pour over the rest of the ingredients. Bake for 45-60 minutes

Rhubarb Crisp

4 C. cut rhubarb
1¼ C. sugar
½ tsp. cinnamon
1 T. flour
¾ C. flour

½ C. oatmeal
½ C. packed brown sugar
½ C. butter
Salt

Place rhubarb in shallow pan. Combine sugar, flour and cinnamon. Sprinkle over fruit. For topping, mix ¾ C. flour, brown sugar and dash of salt. Cut in butter and stir in oatmeal. Sprinkle over fruit and bake at 350° for 1 hour. Makes 8 servings. 345 calories.

October Apple Crisp

1 C. flour
½ C. brown sugar
⅔ C. white sugar
½ C. butter
¼ tsp. salt
4 T. water
10-12 tart apples
Little cinnamon

Mix butter, brown sugar, flour and salt to form crumbly mixture. Butter baking dish and fill ¾ full of sliced apples mixed with white sugar, cinnamon and water. Cover with crumbled mixture and bake at 350° for 45 minutes. Serve with whipped cream.

Oatmeal In Apple Pudding

3 C. sliced apples
½ C. sugar
1 T. flour
1/8 tsp. salt
1/8 tsp. cinnamon
½ C. brown sugar
½ C. flour
½ C. raw oatmeal
1/8 tsp. salt
1/8 tsp. baking powder
¼ C. butter

Combine sliced apples, sugar, flour, salt and cinnamon. Place in baking dish. Crumble with fingers the brown sugar, flour, oatmeal, salt, baking powder and butter. Put on top of first layer and bake at 350° for 30-40 minutes or until apples are tender.

Fruit Cobbler

1 C. sugar
1 T. butter
1 egg
1 C. milk
2 C. flour

2 tsp. baking powder
2 C. fruit
2 C. boiling water or juice
1 C. sugar

Combine sugar, butter, egg, milk, flour and baking powder. Pour in a 9 x 13-inch pan. Mix together fruit, boiling water and sugar. Pour over first layer. Bake at 350° for 30 minutes. Rhubarb is a delicious fruit to use, but any kind of fruit is good.

Cherry Dessert

1 (16-18) pkg. graham crackers, crushed
½ C. melted butter
¼ C. sugar

1 pkg. powdered whipped cream
1 C. powdered sugar
1 (3 oz.) pkg. cream cheese
1 can cherry pie filling

Crush graham crackers, mix in butter and sugar. Place in 9 x 9-inch pan. Second layer: whip cream, add powdered sugar and cream cheese. Whip together and spread over graham crackers. Spread on top the can of cherry pie filling. Chill overnight before serving.

Party Time Pineapple-Coconut Torte

1 pt. whipping cream or 1 pkg.
  Dream Whip, whipped
4 egg whites
1 C. sugar

1 T. Knox gelatin
1 (No. 303) size can crushed
  pineapple
1 pkg. coconut cookies

Beat egg whites stiff; add sugar gradually. Add well drained pineapple. Dissolve gelatin in a little cold water, add enough hot water to make ½ C. Whip cream stiff. Crush part of cookies, line pan. Pour half of mixture, then lay whole cookies in a layer. Finish wiht rest of pineapple mixture. Sprinkle crushed cookies over top.

Apple Cake

2 C. dry bread crumbs
½ C. butter
2 T. sugar

2½ C. sweet applesauce
½ pt. whipping cream

The crumbs are best when made of dried French bread. Roll or grind them very fine. Mix with sugar. Melt butter in a heavy skillet and stir in the bread crumbs. Stir carefully to prevent burning until all the butter is absorbed and the crumbs are crisp and brown. Cool. Place a layer in the bottom of a buttered pan; cover with a layer of applesauce. Repeat until you have sereral layers of applesauce and crumbs and all the ingredients have been used with a layer of crumbs on top. Place in refrigerator for several hours before serving. Serve with whipped cream and dash of red jelly.

Oreo Dessert

1 sm. pkg. Oreos, crushed
½ gal. softened mint ice cream
8 oz. whipped cream

1 jar Smuckers chocolate fudge
  topping

Crush cookies, put into 9 × 13-inch pan; pat down. Freeze 20 minutes. Put ice cream on top. Freeze 20 minutes. Spread chocolate fudge on top. Freeze 20 minutes. Cover with whipped cream.

Chocolate Cherry Creams

1 (6 oz.) pkg. semi-sweet chocolate
  morsels
½ C. evaporated milk
2½ C. powdered sugar, sifted

⅓ C. nuts, chopped
⅓ C. maraschino cherries, cut-up
1¼ C. coconut, cut-up

Put semi-chocolate morsels and evaporated milk into a heavy 2 qt. saucepan. Stir over low heat until chocolate melts completely. Remove from heat. Stir in sifted powdered sugr, mix well, chopped nuts and well drained cut-up maraschino cherries. Chill until mixture is firm enough to handle, about 1 hour. Roll teaspoonfuls of mixture into the cut-up coconut. Chill until firm, about 4 hours. Makes 30.

Apple Dessert

2 qts. slices apples
2 C. sugar
2 T. flour
1 tsp. cinnamon
2 C. oatmeal

2 C. flour
2 C. brown sugar
½ tsp. soda
1 tsp. baking powder
5 T. melted butter

Combine first 4 ingredients, mix good and put in greased pan or dish. Mix remaining ingredients together in dish and put over apple mixture. Bake at 350° for 30-40 minutes in 9 × 12-inch pan, greased. Serves 12.

Can't Wait Cherry Cobbler

2 C. flour
2 C. sugar
4 level tsp. baking powder
Dash of salt

1⅓ C. milk
3 C. fresh cherries
1¼ C. sugar

Mix first 5 ingredients and pour in a greased 9 x 13-inch pan. Pour cherries on top of this. Sprinkle sugar over cherries. Bake at 325° for 45-55 minutes. Serve with ice cream.

Strawberry Graham Cracker Dessert

15 graham crackes
¼ C. sugar
½ C. milk
⅓ C. melted butter
½ C. chopped nuts (opt.)

½ lb. marshmallows
1 C. whipping cream
1 pt. (2 C.) sweetened strawberries

Roll graham crackers fine and add melted butter and sugar. Mix well and pat into greased baking dish. Reserve 2 T. cracker crumbs for top. Melt marshmallows in top of double boiler with milk. Cool this mixture. Add cream which has been whipped. Place layer of marshmallow mixture in dish and then the strawberries and nuts mixed lightly together. Add remaining marshmallow mixture and top with reseved cracker crumbs.

Special Cake Squares

½ lb. butter
½ C. sugar
1 egg yolk
½ tsp. salt
2½ C. flour

4 egg whites
1 C. sugar
1 tsp. vanilla
1 can cherry pie filling
Chopped nuts

Cream butter and sugar; add egg yolk, then flour. Press into a 10×15-inch cake pan. beat 4 egg whites until stiff. Add 1 C. sugar, 1 tsp. vanilla. Beat to a meringue. Pour over dough mixture, the cherry pie filling, then cover with meringue, sprinkled with nuts. Bake at 350° for 40 minutes.

Spice Cake

1 C. sugar
1/2 C. butter
1 egg
1 tsp. cinnamon
1 1/2 C. flour

1 T. cocoa
1 C. sour milk
1 tsp. soda
1 tsp. cloves

Cream sugar and butter. Add egg and beat. Add dry ingredients alternately with sour milk. Bake in 8" X 10" X 2" pan at 350° for 30 minutes. Spread with topping and brown under broiler.

Topping

5 T. melted butter
5 T. cream
7 T. brown sugar
3/4 C. coconut
1/4 C. chopped nuts
1/2 tsp. vanilla

Mom's Fruit Cobbler

2 lg. cans fruit, peaches, pears, apples or apricots
1 C. flour
1 C. sugar
1 tsp. baking powder
½ tsp. salt
1 egg
½ C. melted butter
1 tsp. cinnamon or nutmeg

Put fruit in 9×13-inch pan. Mix flour, sugar, baking powder and salt. Mix well. Break 1 unbeaten egg into the mixture, mix until crumbly. Sprinkle over the top. Melt butter and pour over the top. Sprinkle cinnamon or nutmeg over all. Bake at 350° for 1½ hours.

Apple Crisp

¾ C. sugar
½ tsp. cinnamon
1 C. flour
1⅓ C. flour
½ C. butter

Slice skinned apples in a pie pan about half full. Spread sguar and cinnamon over them; mix. Mix flour, brown sugar and butter together. Spread over apples. Bake at 375° for 30-40 minutes.

BARS and COOKIES

BARS AND COOKIES

Aunt Belle's Brownies 163
Aunt Joy's Sugar Cookies 167
Best Sugar Cookies 168
Big Cookie 180
Brown Bag Cookies 173
Brown Brownies 166
Brownies 163
Butter Cookies 173
Cake Cookies 172
Cake-Cookie Bars 166
Candy Cane Cookies 177
Chocolate Drop Cookies 184
Coconut Bars 187
Cornmeal Balls 178
Date Cookies 175
Easy Sugar Cookies 169
Edna's Peanut Bars 185
Fruited Shortbread Cookies 188
Ginger Cookies 174
Goin' On A Picnic Cake Mix 173
Good Old Cheese Surprise 171
Graham Cracker Bars 165
Grandma's Oatmeal Cookies 175
Honey Cookies 179
Iced Apple Brownies 164
Jus' Plain Sugar Cookies 161
Large Cookies 180
Lisa's Sugar Cookies 168
Marilyn's Cookie Bars 187
Molasses Cookies 181
Mom's Lemon Crumb Squares 186
More Sugar Cookies 171
Neighborly Tea Cakes 178
No Bake Cookies 179
No Bake Corn Flake Cookies 179
Oatmeal Cookies 170, 176, 177
Oatmeal Crispies 185
Oatmeal Crispies Ice Box Cookies 171

- 158 -

BARS AND COOKIES-CONTINUED

Oatmeal Drops 176
Oh Henry Bars 164
Old Fashioned Oatmeal Cookies 181
Orange Slice Cookies 184
Pat's Brownies 162
Pay Day Chocolate Brownies 186
Peanut Butter Cookies 183
Peanut Butter Chip Chocolate Cookies 183
Peanut Butter Unbaked Cookies 169
Real Good Brownies 161
Rhubarb Cookies 174
So-Good Pineapple Bars 165
Sugar Cookies 167, 169, 170, 172, 182
Sugar Drop Cookies 182
Vera's Cookies 162

Jus' Sugar Cookies

1 C. butter
3 eggs
3 C. flour
½ tsp. vanilla

1½ C. sugar
1 tsp. soda and 1 t. warm water
½ tsp. salt

Cream butter and sugar. Add eggs, vanilla, salt and soda. Add in flour. Roll out dough. For frosting, 1 T. Karo syrup and 1 egg yolk adding vanilla, milk and powdered sugar to desired texture and taste.

Real Good Brownies

¼ lb. butter
1 C. white sugar
4 eggs
½ C. chopped nuts

1 tsp. vanilla
1 can Hershey chocolate syrup
1 C. flour
½ tsp. baking powder

FROSTING:
6 T. butter
6 T. milk

1½ C. sugar
½ C. chocolate chips

For first part beat together butter and sugar. Add eggs 2 at a time; beat well. Add remaining ingredients. Spread in greased pan (jelly roll or cookie sheet). Bake at 350° for 30 minutes. Frost as soon as taken out. For frosting, bring butter, milk, sugar to boil in pan. Boil 30 seconds. Remove from heat. Add chocolate chips. Beat a little. Spread on cake.

Vera's Cookies

¼ lb. butter
1 C. graham crackers
1 C. coconut
1 C. nuts
1 C. chocolate chips
1 can Eagle Brand milk

Melt butter in 9 x 13-inch pan. Sprinkle graham crackers over butter; add coconut, nuts, chocolate bits and drizzle milk over top of mixture. Bake at 350° for 30 minutes. Cut while warm.

Pat's Brownies

1 pkg. German chocolate cake mix
⅓ C. evaporated milk
¾ C. melted butter
1 bag walnut pieces
1 (12 oz.) bag semi-sweet chocolate chips
1 bag caramels
⅓ C. evaporated milk

Mix cake mix, ⅓ C. evaporated milk, butter and walnuts. Melt caramels and ⅓ C. evaporated milk. Press half of cake mix mixture into greased floured pan, 9 x 13-inch. Bake at 350° for 7 minutes. Sprinkle chocolate chips over top. Pour the melted caramels and milk mixture over the chocolate chips. Take the other half of top mixture and crumble over top of caramel. Bake for 7 minutes more. Don't overbake or they will get hard.

Brownies

4 eggs   ¼ lb. butter
Beat together. Add:
1½ C. flour   1 lg. can Hershey syrup

Bake 30 minutes or until done at 350°.

FROSTING:
6 T. milk   6 T. butter
1½ C. sugar

Boil 30 seconds. Add ½ C. chocolate chips; beat. Put on cake while hot.

Aunt Belle's Brownies

1½ C. sifted flour   1 C. softened butter
8 T. cocoa   4 unbeaten eggs
1 tsp. salt   2 tsp. vanilla
2 C. sugar   1 C. nuts (opt.)

Preheat oven to 325°. Grease the bottom and sides of an oblong glass baking dish. Combine dry ingredients. Combine butter, eggs, and sugar; mix. Add dry ingredients, vanilla and nuts; mix. Batter will be thick. Pour into baking dish spreading evenly. Bake for 30-35 minutes. Do Not Overbake. Frost with your favorite frosting or sprinkle with powdered sugar.

Oh Henry Bars

4 C. quick oatmeal
½ tsp. salt
½ C. white Karo syurp

⅔ C. butter, melted
1 C. brown sugar

TOPPING:
1 (12 oz.) pkg. chocolate chips
¾ C. peanut butter

Mix ingredients and pour in well greased 9 x 13-inch pan. Bake at 425° for 10 minutes. Cool. Melt chocolate chips and peanut butter. Pour on top and let set.

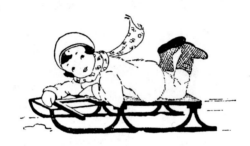

Iced Apple Brownies

3 eggs
1¾ C. sugar
1 C. oil
1 tsp. cinnamon
1 C. chopped nuts

2 C. flour
1 tsp. salt
1 tsp. baking soda
1 C. finely chopped apples

ICING:
¼ C. butter
1 (3 oz.) pkg. cream cheese, softened

1 C. nuts, finely chopped
½ (8 oz.) box powdered sugar
1 tsp. vanilla

Cream eggs with sugar and oil. Add cinnamon and nuts. Stir in dry ingredients and apples. Pour into a 9 x 13-inch pan, greased and bake in 350° preheated oven for 35-40 minutes. For icing, beat all ingredients with a mixer until smooth. Spread on cooled brownies.

Graham Cracker Bars

½ C. butter
1 C. brown sugar
1 C. crushed graham crackers

⅓ C. milk
1 C. flaked coconut

Cook 5 minutes, stir all the time. Spread between layers of graham crackers. Top with powdered sugar and cocoa frosting. Cut into bars.

So Good Pineapple Bars

2 eggs
20 oz. crushed pineapple, undrained
2 C. all-purpose flour

1 C. granulated sugar
1 C. brown sugar
2 tsp. baking soda
1 C. chopped nuts

Beat eggs until light and fluffy. Add next 5 ingredients. Mix well by hand. (If you use an electric mixer too much air gets beaten in.) Stir in nuts and spread batter in an ungreased 9 x 13-inch pan. Bake at 350° for 45-50 minutes. After cake cool, frost with a cream cheese frosting or just sprinkle with powdered sugar.

Cake-Cookie Bars

2 C. brown sugar, packed
2 C. white flour
½ C. butter
1 egg
1 C. chocolate chips

1 tsp. salt
1 tsp. soda
1 C. milk
1 tsp. vanilla
½ C. nutmeats, chopped

Mix together brown sugar, flour and butter. Reserve 1 C. of this mixture. Beat egg and beat in salt, soda, vanilla and milk. Add to brown sugar mixture; mix well. Pour batter into greased 9 x 13-inch pan. Top batter with reserved cup of brown sugar crumbs, to which has been added the chopped nuts. Sprinkle the chocolate chips over the batter and crumbs. Bake at 350° for 30-35 minutes. Cut into bars.

Brown Brownies

½ C. butter
3 T. cocoa
1 C. sugar
¼ tsp. salt

1 tsp. vanilla
1 C. flour
½ tsp. baking powder
½ C. nuts

In small pan melt butter and cocoa, cool. Mix remaining ingredients. Add butter/cocoa mixture and mix well. Pour in greased 8-inch pan. Bake at 350° for 20 minutes. Don't overbake. Frost while hot with fudge frosting.

Aunt Joy's Sugar Cookies

1 C. white sugar
1 C. butter
1 egg
¼ tsp. salt
3½ C. flour

1 tsp. soda
5 T. sour cream or buttermilk
1 tsp. vanilla
½ tsp. almond flavoring

Cream butter and sugar; add egg, salt and flavorings, mix well. Add soda to sour cream or buttermilk and blend well. Add sour cream and flour alternately to creamed mixture; mix well. Chill dough for several hours, then roll out and cut with cookie cutters. Sprinkle with sugar. Bake at 350° until lightly browned.

Sugar Cookies

1 C. Crisco
1 C. butter
1 C. powdered sugar
1 C. white sugar
2 eggs, beaten

2 tsp. vanilla
1 tsp. soda
1 tsp. cream of tartar
4 C. flour, sifted
½ tsp. salt

Mix all together and chill the dough. Make into small balls, roll in sugar. Press down with a fork and bake at 350° for 10-12 minutes. You may add coconut or nutmeg, if desired.

Best Sugar Cookies

1 C. powdered sugar
1 C. butter
2 eggs
1 tsp. salt
1 tsp. cream of tartar

1 C. granulated sugar
1 C. vegetable oil
1 tsp. vanilla
1 tsp. soda
4 C. flour

Cream sugars, butter and oil. Add egg, mix until fluffy. Add dry ingredients, mix well. Roll dough into balls the size of walnuts. Place on ungreased cookie sheet and press with glass dipped in sugar. Bake at 350° for 10 minutes.

Lisa's Sugar Cookies

1¾ C. white sugar
1½ C. lard
2 eggs
1 C. sweet or sour milk
1 level tsp. baking powder

2 rounded tsp. baking powder
1 tsp. vanilla
1 tsp. lemon juice
Pinch of salt
5 C. (approx.) flour

Mix all ingredients together and use just enough flour to make a soft dough. May take more but only use enough to handle dough. Refrigerate for a few hours or overnight, roll out. Bake at 400°, but if cookies spread out use more flour.

Easy Sugar Cookies

1½ C. sugar
1 C. butter
2 egg yolks
1 tsp. cream of tartar

1 tsp. soda
2 C. flour
1 tsp. vanilla

Cream sugar and butter. Add egg yolks and beat well. Sift together cream of tartar, soda, flour and 2 pinches of salt and add to creamed mixture. Stir in vanilla. Form dough into small balls, then roll in white or colored sugar. Bake at 350° for 12-15 minutes.

Peanut Butter Unbaked Cookies

1 C. white sugar
1 C. white corn syrup

2 C. peanut butter
4 C. cornflakes

Mix the white sugar, corn syrup and heat to boiling. Remove from stove and add the peanut butter and stir together. Pour cornflakes in a large bowl and gradually stir in the peanut butter mixture. Drop by teaspoon on cookie sheet and cool.

Sugar Cookies

1 C. granulated sugar
1 C. powdered sugar
1 C. butter
1 C. oil
2 eggs, well beaten

2 tsp. vanilla
1 tsp. cream of tartar
1 tsp. soda
5¼ C. flour

Cream sugars with butter; add beaten eggs. Stir in oil and vanilla. Mix dry ingredients and blend in. Form into balls. Dip in granulated sugar and flatten with bottom of glass. Bake at 350° until lightly browned, 8-10 minutes.

Oatmeal Cookies

¾ C. vegetable shortening
½ C. brown sugar
½ C. granulated sugar
1 egg
1 tsp. vanilla

1 C. flour
1 tsp. salt
½ tsp. baking soda
1 C. raisins
3 C. rolled oats, quick cooking or regular

Preheat oven to 350°. Beat together shortening, sugars, egg, water and vanilla until creamy. Combine flour, salt and soda. Add to creamed mixture. Add raisins and rolled oats; mix well. Drop by rounded teaspoonfuls onto ungreased cookie sheet. Bake for 12-15 mintues. Makes 5 dozen cookies.

Sugar Cookies

¾ C. sugar
⅓ C. shortening
⅓ C. oil
1 T. milk
2 tsp. almond extract

1 egg
1½ C. flour
1½ tsp. baking powder
¼ tsp. salt
Sugar to sprinkle on top

Heat oven to 375°. In large bowl, cream together sugar, shortening, oil, milk, almond extract and egg. Cream until light and fluffy. Stir in dry ingredients and blend well. Spread evenly in ungreased 15 x 10-inch jelly roll pan. Sprinkle with sguar. Bake for 12 minutes or until light brown. Cool 5 minutes and cut into squares or use your favorite cookie cutters.

More Sugar Cookies

1 C. butter
1 C. salad oil
2 C. sugar
2 eggs
½ tsp. salt

2 tsp. vanilla
5 C. flour
2 tsp. soda
2 tsp. cream of tartar

Mix together and chill. Make walnut-size balls and flatten with bottom of glass dipped in sugar. Bake 10 minutes at 350°.

Oatmeal Crispies Ice Box Cookies

1 C. shortening
1 C. brown sugar
1 C. white sugar
2 beaten eggs
1 tsp. vanilla

1½ C. flour
1 tsp. salt
1 tsp. soda
3 C. quick oatmeal
½ C. chopped nuts

Cream sugars and shortening. Add eggs and vanilla and beat well. Add dry ingredients and nuts. Shape in 2 rolls, wrap in waxed paper and chill overnight. Slice thin and bake at 350° about 10 minutes.

Good Old Cheese Surprise

8 oz. cottage cheese
1 C. soft butter
2 C. flour

¼ stick melted butter
¾ C. shopped walnuts
¾ C. brown sugar

Blend cheese and butter. Mix in flour to form dough. Roll out into 3 sections as for pie crust. Sprinkle with nuts and brown sugar. Roll as is or cut into pre-shaped wedges. Bake at 375° for 15-20 minutes on greased and floured cookie sheet. Sprinkle with powdered sugar.

Sugar Cookies

6 C. flour
2 C. sugar
3 tsp. baking powder
1 tsp. salt

2 C. butter
2 eggs, beaten
½ C. light cream or milk
2 tsp. vanilla

In mixing bowl, stir together dry ingredients. Cut in butter until mixture looks like coarse crumbs. Add egg, cream and vanilla; mix well. On "lightly" floured surface roll out dough to ¼-inch thick. Cut with cookie cutter. Place on greased sheet. Bake at 400° for 7-8 minutes or until "just" starting to brown.

Cake Cookies

Cake mix
⅓ C. oil

1 tsp. vanilla
2 eggs

Combine ½ of cake mix with other ingredients; mix well. Add rest of mix. If you wish, add nut meats, raisins, chocolate bits or butterscotch bits. Drop by teaspoon on slightly greased cookie sheet. Bake in preheated 350° oven for 8 minutes for chewy; 10 minutes for crisp.

Brown Bag Cookies

1 C. sugar
1 C. brown sugar
1 C. butter
2 eggs
2 tsp. vanilla

2 C. rolled oats
2 C. flour
2 C. cornflakes
2 tsp. soda
½ tsp. salt

Cream together the sugars, butter, eggs and vanilla. Shake together all the dry ingredients in brown bag. (Raisins, coconut, chocolate chips and nuts may be added to dry ingredients.) Add dry mixture to creamed mixture. Drop by teaspoonful on a greased baking sheet and bake in a 350° oven for 10 minutes.

Goin' On A Picnic Cake Mix Cookies

1 lg. box cake mix
2 eggs
½ tsp. soda

½ C. butter, melted
½ C. flour

Beat all ingredients together. Roll in ball. Place about 1-inch apart on ungreased cookie sheet. Bake at 350° for 10 minutes.

Butter Cookies

1¾ C. flour
½ tsp. baking powder
⅔ C. butter

½ C. sugar
1 sm. egg, well beaten
½ tsp. vanilla

Sift flour with baking powder. Cream butter well; add sugar and continue creaming until well mixed. Mix in the beaten egg. Add vanilla. Stir in sifted dry ingredients in 2 or 3 portions until dough is just smooth. Roll out to 1/8-inch thick on a floured surface and cut into desired shapes. Bake on ungreased cookie sheet in a moderately hot oven, 400° for 6-8 minutes or until delicately browned. Makes 3-4 dozen cookies.

Ginger Cookies

2½ C. flour
½ tsp. salt
1 tsp. cinnamon
1 C. brown sugar
¼ C. molasses
¼ C. sugar

2 tsp. baking soda
3 tsp. ginger
¾ C. butter
1 egg
1 T. lemon rind or 2 tsp. lemon juice

Preheat oven to 350°. Mix flour, soda, salt, ginger and cinnamon in bowl. Cream butter, brown sugar and egg in another bowl until fluffy. Beat in molasses and lemon rind. Stir in dry ingredients, half at a time; blend well after each time. Roll level teaspoonfuls on dough between palms into balls; roll in sugar. Place on ungreased cookie sheet. Bake for 10 minutes.

Rhubarb Cookies

½ C. shortening
1 C. brown sugar
1 egg
½ tsp. salt
½ tsp. cinnamon
¼ tsp. cloves
½ tsp. nutmeg

2 C. flour
1 tsp. baking soda
¼ C. milk
1 C. chopped nuts
1 C. raisins
1 C. finely chopped rhubarb
¼ C. flaked coconut

Cream shortening and sugar. Add egg and mix well. Sift together dry ingredients and add alternately with milk. Fold in nuts, raisins, rhubarb and coconut. Drop by teaspoons on greased cookie sheets. Bake at 375° for 10-12 minutes. Makes 4½ dozen.

Grandma's Oatmeal Cookies

2 C. brown sugar
2 C. oatmeal
2 C. flour
½ C. shortening
½ C. butter

2 eggs, beaten
1 tsp. soda
2 T. hot water
1 C,. ground dates
½ C. nuts

Mix shortening and butter together. Mix sugar, oatmeal, flour and shortening cutting until pea size. Dissolve soda in hot water; add eggs. Mix and add to first mixture. Add dates and nuts. You may refrigerate dough. Pat dough out and cut. Bake at 375° for 5-10 minutes.

Date Cookies

1 C. white sugar
1 C. brown sugar
1 C. shortening
3 eggs

¼ tsp. salt
1 tsp. soda
4 C. flour
1 tsp. vanilla

Boil 1 lb. chopped date, ¾ C. sugar and 1 C. hot water; let cool. Add ½ C. nutmeats chopped. Cream sugar and shortening. Add well beaten eggs and mix well. Dissolve soda in 2 T. hot water and add to sugar, etc. Add vanilla. Put the salt in flour and sift into batter a little at a time; mix well. Divide the cookie dough into 2 equal parts and roll each part into a rectangle shape ¼-inch thick. Spread the cooled date filling over the 2 rectangles. Roll up as a jelly roll. Place in pan and chill 3 hours or overnight. Slice in 3/8-inch slices. Bake at 350° for 20 minutes.

Oatmeal Drops

1 C. sugar
1 C. shortening
1 tsp. cinnamon
1 tsp. soda
1 C. raisins
7 T. liquid

2 eggs
2 C. oatmeal
2 C. flour
2 tsp. vanilla
1 tsp. salt
1 C. nuts, chopped

Boil raisins in water so as to have 7 T. liquid left. Cool. Cream sugar and shortening; add other ingredients. Drop by spoonful onto greased cookie sheet. Bake at 375° for 12-15 minutes or until desired brownies.

Oatmeal Cookies

2 C. quick cooking oats
2 C. firmly packed brown sugar
1 tsp. almond extract

1 tsp. salt
1 C. salad oil

Drop by teaspoonfuls 2-inches apart, on a greased cookie sheet. Bake at 325° for 15 minutes. Store in tight covered container.

Oatmeal Cookies

1 C. butter
1 C. brown sugar
1 egg
1 tsp. vanilla

1 tsp. soda dissolved in 2 tsp. hot water
1½ C. flour sifted
2½ C. oatmeal

Cream the butter and sugar. Add the egg and vanilla; beat well. Mix the flour and oatmeal, stir into the creamed mixture along with the soda. Roll into balls the size of walnuts and flatten on cookie sheet. Bake at 375° for 15 minutes.

Candy Cane Cookies

1 C. shortening, half butter
1 C. sifted confectioner's sugar
1 egg

1 tsp. vanilla
1½ tsp. almond extract

Preheat oven to 375°. Mix all ingredients thoroughly. Sift together and stir in 2½ C. sifted flour, 1 tsp. salt. Divide dough in two halves. Blend into one half ½ tsp. red food coloring. Roll 1 tsp. each color dough into a strip about 4-inches long. Place strips side by side; press together and twist like a rope. Place on ungreased cookie sheet. Curve to down to form cane handle. Bake 9 minutes until brown. Roll in mixture ½ C. sugar, ½ C. crushed peppermint candy.

Neighborly Tea Cakes

1 C. butter
2¼ C. sifted flour
1 tsp. vanilla

½ C. powdered sugar
¼ tsp. salt
¾ C. finely chopped nuts

Cream butter and powdered sugar. Add rest of ingredients. Bake on ungreased cookie sheet, teaspoon size balls, 14-17 minutes at 350°.

Cornmeal Balls

½ tsp. cornmeal
2 tsp. salt
2 C. milk
¾ C. sugar
¾ C. shortening

2 eggs, beaten
2 pkgs. yeast
1 C. warm water
5-6 C. flour

Cook cornmeal, salt and milk until thick. While still hot add the sugar and shortening; cool. Dissolve yeast in warm water and mix well with cornmeal mixture. Add eggs and stir. Stir in 5-6 C. flour to make medium dough. Knead, put in greased bowl and let rise for about an hour. Divide dough into 6 equal parts. Roll each part into a circle. Brush with melted butter. Cut into 8 pieces pie wedged. Start at large end to roll up and place on greased pan. Let rise for about 45 minutes. Bake at 350° for 12-15 minutes or until lightly brown.

Honey Cookies

1 C. honey
3¾ C. flour
4¾ tsp. baking powder
¼ tsp. baking soda

1 C. shortening, Crisco or lard
½ tsp. each: cinnamon, cloves and allspice

Heat honey and shortening together about 1 minutes; cool. Sift flour, baking powder and soda; also spices together. Add to first mixture to make a soft dough. Roll thin, cut and bake at 350° for 12-15 minutes. Yield: 6 dozen cookies. Frost with powdered sugar frosting.

No Bake Corn Flake Cookies

½ C. white Karo
½ C. white sugar
2 T. cocoa

½ C. peanut butter
3 C. cornflakes

Place Karo, sugar and cocoa in saucepan and bring to a boil. Then remove from heat. Stir in peanut butter and cornflakes. Drop on waxed paper to cool.

No Bake Cookies

2 C. white sugar
½ C. milk

¼-½ C. cocoa
¼ C. butter

Cook for 12 minutes, then remove from heat and add:

½ C. chunky peanut butter
3 C. oatmeal

1 tsp. vanilla

Drop by spoonfuls on waxed paper to cool. Makes 2 dozen.

Big Cookie

1 T. peanut butter
2 T. + 2 tsp. non-fat dry milk
2 T. raisins
½ tsp. baking powder
2 T. water

2 tsp. brown sugar or honey or sugar substitute
¾ oz. oatmeal, uncooked, old fashioned

Preheat oven to 350°. In medium bowl combine all ingredients. Spray cookie sheet with Pam, drop mixture on sheet. Bake 10 minutes. Equals one serving.

Large Cookies

2 C. sugar
1 C. shortening
2 eggs
1 C. sour milk, buttermilk

2 tsp. vanilla
3½ C. flour
2 tsp. soda
½ tsp. salt

Mix together and drop by large spoonful onto cookie sheet. Bake 15 minutes at 375°.

Old Fashioned Oatmeal Cookies

1 C. raisins
1 C. water
¾ C. shortening
1½ C. sugar
2 eggs
1 tsp. vanilla
2½ C. flour

1 tsp. soda
1 tsp. salt
1 tsp. cinnamon
½ tsp. baking powder
½ tsp. cloves
2 C. oats
½ C. chopped nuts

Simmer raisins and water over medium heat until raisins are plump about 15 minutes. Drain raisins, reserving the liquid. Add enough water if needed to measure ½ cup. Heat oven to 400°. Mix thoroughly shortening, sugar, eggs and vanilla. Stir in reserved liquid. Blend in remaining ingredients. Drop dough by rounded teaspoonsful about 2-inches apart onto greased baking sheet. Bake 8-10 minutes or until brown. About 6½ dozen cookies.

Molasses Cookies

1 C. lard
1 C. sugar
1 egg
½ C. hot water
1 C. molasses

2 tsp. soda
½ tsp. ginger
½ tsp. cloves
5½ C flour, about

Cream lard and sugar. Add egg, molasses and water and blend well. Stir flour, soda, ginger and cloves and add to the above. Refrigerate for 1 hour or overnight. Roll out on floured board to about ¼-inch thick and cut with favorite cookie cutter. Bake at 400° for about 10 minutes. May be frosted or stored in tighly covered container.

Sugar Drop Cookies

2 C. sugar
1 C. shortening
1 tsp. vanilla
½ C. milk

4 C. flour
½ tsp. salt
1 tsp. soda
1 tsp. baking powder

Cream shortening and sugar; add 2 beaten eggs. Then add milk, vanilla and dry ingredients. May add nuts. Drop by spoonfuls on greased cookies sheet. Bake at 350° for 8-10 minutes. This can be kept in the ice box for several days, then rolled in balls and flatten with spoon or something wiht design on it.

Sugar Cookies

CREAM TOGETHER:
1 C. sugar
1 C. butter
Add 2 eggs

1 C. powdered sugar
1 C. oil

SIFT TOGETHER:
4½ C. flour
1 tsp. cream of tartar

1 tsp. baking soda
1 tsp. vanilla, last

Refrigerate overnight. Roll in balls and roll in sugar and press with a fork. Bake.

Peanut Butter Chip Chocolate Cookies

1 C. butter
1½ C. sugar
2 eggs
2 tsp. vanilla
2 C. unsifted all-purpose flour

⅔ C. Hershey's cocoa
¾ tsp. baking soda
½ tsp. salt
2 C. (12 oz. pkg) peanut butter chips

Cream butter, sugar, eggs and vanilla until light and fluffy. Combine flour, cocoa, baking soda and salt; add to creamed mixture. Stir in peanut butter chips. Chill until firm enough to handle. Shape small amounts of dough into 1-inch balls. Place on ungreased baking sheet and flatten slightly with fork. Bake at 350° for 8-10 minutes. Cool 1 minutes before sheet onto wire rack. Makes about 6 dozen 2½-inch cookies.

Peanut Butter Cookies

2½ C. unsifted flour
1 tsp. baking soda
1 C. butter
1 C. brown sugar
1 tsp. vanilla

1 tsp. baking powder
¼ tsp. salt
1 C. peanut butter, creamy or chunky
2 eggs

Mix first 4 ingredients; set aside. Beat butter, peanut butter, then add sugar, eggs and vanilla. Add flour mixture, beat until well blened. Chill dough. Shape into 1-inch balls. Place on ungreased cookie sheet; flatten slightly. Bake at 350° for 12 minutes or until lightly browned. Makes 6 dozen cookies.

Chocolate Drop Cookies

1 C. brown sugar
1 egg
½ tsp. baking soda
1½ C. flour
½ C. chopped nutmeats

½ C butter
3 tsp. cocoa
1 tsp. baking powder
½ C. sour cream
½ tsp. vanilla

Combine all ingredients and drop by teaspoonful on a greased baking sheet. Bake at 350° for 10 minutes. Makes 3½ dozens.

Orange Slice Cookies

1½ C. brown sugar
½ C. shortening
2 eggs
2 C. flour
1 tsp. soda

½ tsp. salt
1 lb. orange slice candy
½ C. flaked coconut or nuts
½ C. quick oatmeal

Cream sugar and shortening. Beat in eggs. Sift 1½ C. flour, soda and salt. Blend into creamed mixture. Cut orange slices into small pieces and mix with remaining ½ C. flour. Add with remaining ingredients. Drop by teaspoon onto greased cookie sheet. Bake at 325° for 10-12 minutes. Yields: 5 dozen.

Oatmeal Crispies

1 C. shortening
1 C. brown sugar
1 C. white sugar
2 eggs, well beaten
1½ C. flour

1 tsp. vanilla
1 tsp. salt
1 tsp. soda
3 C. quick oatmeal
½ C. nuts

Mix in oder. Bake at 350° for 10 minutes.

Edna's Peanut Butter

3 eggs
1½ C sugar
2 C. flour
1 C. cold water
2 tsp. baking powder

½ tsp. salt
1 tsp. vanilla
Ground peanuts
Powdered sugar

Beat eggs about 2 minutes. Add sugar and beat 5 minutes. Add 1 C. flour and beat well. Add water, baking powder and second cup of flour; beat. Add salt and vanilla. Bake in moderate oven about 30 minutes. Springs back to touch when done. Cut into small bars. Make a thin milk and powdered sugar frosting, about the consistency of whipping cream. Dip each bar in the frosting and roll in ground peanuts.

Pay Day Chocolate Brownies

¾ C. cocoa
½ tsp. soda
⅔ C. butter, melted
½ C. boiling water
1½ C. sugar

2 eggs
1⅓ C flour
½ tsp. salt
1 tsp. vanilla

Mix cocoa and soda. Blend in ⅓ C. butter. Add ½ C. boiling water. Stir this until it thickens. Stir in sugar, eggs and remaining ⅓ C. butter. Stir until smooth. Add flour, vanilla and salt. Bake at 350° in a 9 x 13-inch pan for 20-25 minutes.

Mom's Lemon Crumb Squares

1 can sweetened milk
½ C. lemon juice
1 tsp. lemon peel
1½ C. flour
1 tsp. baking powder

½ tsp. salt
⅔ C. butter
1 C. brown sugar
1 C. uncooked oatmeal

Blend together condensed milk, juice and lemon peel. Cream butter; add sugar and blend well. Add oatmeal. Sift flour, baking powder and salt. Add to oatmeal mixture. Mix until crumbly. Put in pan and spread. Save some of crumb mixture. Spread lemon mixture on top. Cover with rest of crumb mixture. Bake at 350° for 25 minutes until brown around edges. Cool in pan for 15 mintues. Cut into squares and chill in pan until firm.

Marilyn's Cookie Bars

1½ C. cornflakes crumbs
3 T. sugar
½ C. butter, melted
1 C. (6 oz. pkg.) semi-sweet chocolate morsels

1⅓ C. (3½ oz. can) flaked coconut
1 C. coarsely chopped walnuts
1 can Borden's Eagle Brand sweetened condensed milk, not not evaporated milk

Measure cornflake crumbs, sugar and butter into 9 x 13-inch baking pan; mix thoroughly. With back of tablespoon, press mixture evenly and firmly in bottom of pan to form crust. Scatter chocolate morsels over crust. Spread coconut evenly over chocolate morsels. Sprinkle the walnuts over the coconut. Pour sweetened condensed milk evenly over the walnuts. Bake at 350° about 25 minutes.

Coconut Bars

½ C. brown sugar, packed
½ C. butter

1 C. flour

Blend like pie crust the first 3 ingredients and spread in 9 x 13-inch pan. Bake 10 minutes at 325°.

1 C. brown sugar
2 T. flour
½ tsp. baking powder
2 eggs, beat well

1 tsp. vanilla
1 C. coconut
1 C. chopped nuts
Pinch of salt

Mix remaining ingredients and spread over top of first mixture. Bake at 350° for 20 minutes

Fruited Shortbread Cookies

2 1/2 C. flour
1 tsp. soda
1 tsp. cream of tarter 1/2 C. butter
1 C. margarine, softened

1 1/2 C. powdered sugar
1 egg
1 (9 oz.) pkg. mincemeat
1 tsp. vanilla

Mix together flour, soda and cream of tarter. In large bowl, mix margarine and sugar. Add egg. Mix well. Stir in crumbled mincemeat and vanilla. Add flour mixture. (Dough will be stiff.) Roll into 1/4-inch balls. Place on ungreased cookie sheet, flatten slightly. Bake for 10 or 12 min. in a 375° oven. Cool. Frost with lemon icing. Garnish with nuts. Makes 3 dozen.

CANDY

CANDY

Anise Candy 197
Bon Bon's 193
Brown Sugar Fudge 193
Caramel Treats 193
Cracker Candy 195
Gumdrop Goodies 191
Divinity 196
Down Home Oven Caramel Corn 195
Leone's Fudge 198
Nut Caramels 194
Old Country Popcorn Balls 196
Peanut Brittle 191,192
Peanut Butter Fudge 197
Peanut Butter Popcorn Balls 196
Popcorn Cake 192
Yummie Fudge 194

Gumdrop Goodies

1⅓ C. applesauce
2 envelopes unflavored gelatin
6 oz. pkg. fruit flavored gelatin

2 C. sugar
1 tsp. lemon juice
Sugar

Mix applesauce, unflavored and flavored gelatins, 2 C. sugar and lemon juice in a saucepan. Heat to boiling and boil 1 minute, stirring constantly. Fill a loaf pan half full with cold water. Pour out water and pour gelatin mixture into wet pan. Clean out saucepan with a rubber scraper. When loaf pan cools enough to touch, refrigerate for about 3 hours or until candy is firm. Cut candy into 1-inch sqaures (dip knife in cold water to keep from sticking.) Lift each square out and place on an ungreased cookie sheet. Let stand 8 hours to dry. After candy is dry, roll in sugar to coat all sides.

Peanut Brittle

2 C. sugar
¼ tsp. salt

1 C. white Karo
1 C. water
3 C. raw peanuts

Cook above to 234° on candy thermometer. Add 3 C. raw peanuts. Cook 8 minutes, stirring all the time. Add 2 T. butter. Cook to 300°. Remove from heat add 1 tsp. vanilla and stir. Add 2 tsp. soda, stir 15 seconds and pour onto buttered cookie sheet to cool. This will foam so use care when handling. After cool, break into pieces.

Peanut Brittle

1 C. white sugar
1 C. white corn syrup
2 C. raw peanuts

Boil all ingredients in deep pan. Boil to 280° on candy thermometer. Remove from heat. Add 1 T. soda, stir. Will foam. Quickly pour onto buttered pan, cool. Break into pieces.

Popcorn Cake

5 qts. popped popcorn
1 lg. bag gumdrops
1 lg. jar peanuts
1 lg. bag (about 30 ct.) marshmallows
¼ C. butter

Have 5 quarts popped popcorn in large pan. Add 1 package gumdrops, 1 large jar peanuts. Melt in a double boiler, 1 large bag marshmallows, ¼ C. butter. Take off stove and pour over popcorn, gumdrops and peanuts. Work quickly. Mix together with long spoon or buttered hands. Spoon into buttered Jello ring mold or bundt pan. Press down so popcorn, peanuts and gumdrops stick together. Allow to cool. Cut into pieces like cake. (Using green and red gumdrops makes a nice popcorn cake at Christmas time.)

Bon Bon's

½ lb. butter
2 boxes (1 lb.) powdered sugar
1 can Eagle Brand condensed milk
1 tsp. vanilla
1 pkg. coconut
1 C. nuts

DIP:
2 (6 oz. ea.) pkgs. chocolate chips   1 slab paraffin

Melt butter; add powdered sugar, condensed milk, vanilla, coconut and nuts. Chill for several hours or overnight. Roll into balls about the size of small walnuts and place on wax paper lined cookie sheets. Put back in ice box until you are ready to dip them. While you are making the balls, melt the chocolate chips and paraffin over hot water and keep it hot while you are dipping. Stick a sharp pointed instrument (nut pick, toothpick, etc.) into bottom of candy (or the top) and dip quickly into the chocolate dip. Roll slightly to cover nicely and place back on wax paper. These store nicely.

Caramel Treats

1 (16 oz.) pkg. caramels
½ lb. butter
1 can Bordens evaporated milk
Marshmallows
rice krispies

Melt caramels and butter in double boiler. When melted, add 1 can of sweetened milk. Put toothpicks in marshmallows and freeze, then dip in caramel and roll in rice krispies.

Nut Caramels

¼ C. butter
1 C. evaporated milk
1 C. sugar
1 C. dark corn syrup

¼ tsp. salt
¼ tsp. vanilla
1 C. pecans

Generously butter an 8-inch square pan. In a small saucepan, heat butter and evaporated milk until butter is melted. In separate 2 quart saucepan cook sugar, corn syrup and salt over medium heat until it reaches firm ball stage, 244°, stirring often. Slowly stir in milk mixture, so sugar mixture does not stop boiling. Stirring constantly, cook mixture until it reaches firm ball stage again. Remove pan from heat and stir in vanilla and pecans; mix well. Pour itno buttered pan. When firm, turn out onto cutting board on wax paper. Cut caramel in 1-inch squares and wrap in plastic wrap. Makes 5 dozen.

Yummie Fudge

1 lb. Velveeta cheese
4 lbs. powdered sugar
1 lb. butter

1 tsp. vanilla
1 C. cocoa
Walnuts, if desired

Melt cheese and butter. Sift together cocoa and powdered sugar. Combine and add vanilla and nuts. Spread fudge mixture on a buttered cookie sheet; let cool.

Down Home Oven Caramel Corn

8-9 qt. popped popcorn
2 C. brown sugar
1 C. butter
1 tsp. salt

½ C. white syrup
1 tsp. burnt sugar or vanilla
½ tsp. soda

Mix all ingredients together, except corn and soda; boil for 5 minutes, mixing well and stirring. Remove from heat and add soda; stir in quickly and pur over popped popcorn, mixing well. Put in 2 large flat pans and place in 250° oven for 1 hour, stirring 2-3 times. Store in tightly closed container.

Cracker Candy

2 C. sugar
½ C. milk
¼ lb. soda crackers, finely crushed

1 heaping tsp. peanut butter
1 tsp. vanilla

Combine sugar and milk; bring to a boil. Add crackers, peanut butter and vanilla. Stir well and let stand for 5 minutes. Beat and pour into a buttered 8x8x2-inch square pan. Cool in ice box. Cut into squares.

Peanut Butter Popcorn Balls

1 C. raw popcorn
1 C. white sugar
1 C. light syrup

1 C. chunky peanut butter
1 tsp. vanilla
1 C. Spanish salted peanuts (opt.)

Pop corn and keep warm in 200° oven. Bring sugar and syrup to a rolling boil, stirring constantly. Remove from heat and add peanut butter and vanilla; mix well. Pour over popcorn and mix well. Form into small balls. Optional: Add peanuts to syrup mixture before pouring over popcorn.

Divinity

4 C. sugar
1 C. light corn syrup
¾ C. water

3 egg whites, beaten
1 tsp. vanilla
½ C. chopped nuts

Combine sugar, light syrup and water; cook over low heat. Stir until sugar is dissolved. Cook without stirring at 225°. Remove from heat and add egg whites, beating constantly. Continue beating until mixture holds its shape and loses its gloss. Add vanilla and nuts. Drop by teaspoonfuls on lightly buttered pan.

Old Country Popcorn Balls

¾ C. white corn syrup
¼ C. honey
½ C. butter
2 tsp. vinegar

1 tsp. vanilla
1½ C. sugar
6-7 qt. popped popcorn

Boil corn syrup, honey, butter, vinegar, vanilla and sguar until it snaps or to the hard boil stage when tested in cold water. Pour over popped popcorn which has been heated in the oven at 250°. Mix well and form into balls, using damp hands to form the balls.

Peanut Butter Fudge

1 C. white sugar
1 C. brown sugar
Pinch of salt
½ C. peanut butter

2 T. butter
1 T. vanilla
1 C. marshmallows
¼ C. evaporated milk

Cook sugar, butter and milk to a soft boil, 240°. Add salt, vanilla and mix. Add marshmallows and peanut butter. Remove from heat and beat until thick. Pour into pan and let stand until hard.

Anise Candy

3 C. sugar
1 C. white syrup
½ C. water

1 tsp. red coloring
1 tsp. anise extract or a few drops anise oil

Boil to hard crack. Add red coloring and anise oil last. Do not stir. Pour in an ungreased pan or cookie sheet. Let harden and break into pieces. Be sure candy has reached the hard crack stage or it will not be brittle enough. When candy is done it will crack when you test it in cold water.

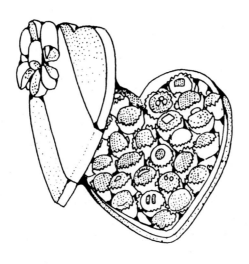

Leona's Fudge

4 C. white sugar
1 (14½ oz.) can evaporated milk
¼ lb. butter
12 oz. pkg. chocolate chips

1 pt. jar marshmallows creme
1 tsp. vanilla
Nuts (opt.)

Cook to soft ball stage the sugar, evaporated milk and butter, stirring constantly. Remove from heat and immediately stir in chocolate chips, marshmallow creme and vanilla. Add nuts and pour at once in 9 x 13-inch buttered pan. Cut when cooled.

Brown Sugar Fudge

2 C. brown sugar
1 C. white sugar
1 C. light cream

½ C. butter
1 tsp. vanilla
1 C. chopped nuts

Combine sugars, cream and butter. Cook to softball stage, 238°, stirring frequently; add vanilla. Cool to lukewarm (110°). Beat till mixture loses its gloss. Stir in nuts and pour into buttered 10 x 6 x 1½-inch pan. Cool and cut in squares.

MISCELLANEOUS

MISCELLANEOUS

Apple Butter 201
Beer Batter 210
Bread 'N Butter Pickles 203
Casserole Sauce Mix 208
Chicken Dressing 209
Cinnamon Pickles 205
Crab Apple Pickles 201
Cucumber Chips 207
Dill Pickles 203,204
Easy Jam 202
Easy Strawberry Jam 208
Helen's Dill Pickles 206
Hurry-Up Hamburger Mix 207
Ice Box Pickles 207
Meat Sauce 208
Pretty Girl Dill Pickles 204
Rhubarb-Raspberry Jam 202
Sweet Pickles 206,210
Zucchini Jam 209

Crab Apple Pickles

1 gal. apples, washed and pricked
5 C. sugar
4 .C dark vinegar
3 C. water

2 sticks cinnamon
1 T. whole allspice
½ T. whole cloves
Gauze bag

In large kettle, mix sugar, vinegar and water. Tie spices in gauze bag and add to syrup mixture. Bring syrup to a boil and cook until sugar dissolves. Remove from heat and cool. When cooled add apples (whole) and return to heat. Simmer until apples are tender but not mushy. Remove from heat and let stand 12-18 hours. Remove apples from syrup and pack into hot jars. Heat syrup and pour over apples, seal with hot lids.

Apple Butter

2 qts. cooked apple pulp
2 tsp. cinnamon

4 C. sugar
¼ tsp. cloves

Measure pulp, add sugar and spices. Cook until flavors are well blended, about 15 minutes, stirring constantly to prevent sticking. Cook until mixture thickens. If too thick, add a small amount of water for desired consistency. Pour hot into hot ball jars, leaving ¼-inch head space. Adjust flats and bands. Process pints and quarts 10 minutes in canner of boiling water.

Easy Jam

1 C. strawberries or raspberries
1 C. sugar

1 tsp. lemon juice (opt.)

Crush enough berries to make 1 C.; add 1 C. sugar and lemon juice. Boil hard for about 1 minute, check by raising spoon, when it coats spoon or form drops on bottom, it has cooked enough. If you want a firmer jam, you can cook it longer. Never double recipe.

Rhubarb-Raspberry Jam

4 C. cut up rhubarb
4 C. sugar

1 pkg. raspberry Jello
1 sm. can crushed pineapple

Let 4 C. rhubarb and sugar stand until it makes its own juice. Then boil 15 minutes. Remove from heat and add 1 package Jello and the pineapple. Pour into jam glasses and refrigerate.

Bread 'N Butter Pickles

1 qt. cider vinegar
1 pt. water
4 C. sugar
⅓ C. salt
Onions

2 tsp. celery seed
2 tsp. mustard seed
⅔ tsp. turmeric
½ tsp. ginger
Large cucumbers

Slice cucumbers in bowl, cover lightly. Refrigerate overnight. The next day, fill jars with sliced cucumbers. Top with several slices of onion. Mix vinegar, water, sugar, salt, celery seed, mustard seed, turmeric and ginger into a large pan. Bring to boil and boil until sugar and salt dissolve. Pour sauce over cucumber until they are covered. If using rubbers and zinc lids, wipe jar off and put lids on and tighten. This is all you have to do to seal these jars. If using flats and bands, wipe jar off, put lids on and tighten. Bring ¾ full canner of water to boil. Add jars and boil for 5 minutes. Remove jars and tighten lids if necessary. Let all jars stand for 6 weeks before using to allow flavors to completely penetrate the cucumbers. Makes 3½-4 quarts.

Dill Pickles

1 C. sugar
1 .C vinegar
2 T. salt

Onion
Dill

Boil first 3 ingredients. Cut onion, Put slice in bottom of jar. Also head of dill. Fill jar with sliced cucumbers. Cover with above mixture and seal. Make sure syrup is real hot.

Pretty-Girl Dill Pickles

3-5-inch cucumbers
2 qt. water
Alum
Dill

1 qt. vinegar
1½ qt. vinegar
Garlic cloves

Arrange cucumbers in fruit jars with 2 cloves garlic, a stalk of dill, and a pinch of alum. In a large pan, combine water, vinegar and salt. Bring to a boil and boil until salt dissolves. Cover cucumbers with hot liquid. If using rubbers and zinc lids, wipe jar off and put lids on and tighten. This is all you have to do to seal these jars. If using flats and bands, wipe jars off, put lids on and tighten. Bring ¾ full canner of water to boil. Add jars and boil for 5 minutes. Remove jars and tighten lids if necessary. Let all jars stand for 6 weeks before using to allow flavors to completely penetrate the cucumbers.

Dill Pickles

Wash cucumbers and pack in hot jars. Add 1-2 heads of dill to each jar. Combine 2 quarts water, 1 quart vinegar and 1 C. pickling salt and boil hard. Pour over cucumbers and seal jars.

Cinnamon Pickles

2 gals. cucumbers 8½ qts. water
2 C. lime

Let stand 24 hours. Drain and rinse. Soak 3 hours in cold water; drain well.

In a large kettle:

1 bottle red food coloring 1 C. vinegar
1 T. alum

Add cucumbers and simmer 2 hours; drain.

SYRUP:
2 C. vinegar 10 C. sugar
2 C. water 1 pkg. cinnamon candies or red hots

Put hot over cucumbers overnight. Repeat 3 days. On third day pack in jars. Pour hot syrup over and seal.

Helen's Dill Dandies

2 C. white vinegar
6 C. water
⅓ C. (scant) canning salt
Garlic

Bring vinegar, salt and water to boil. Pour into cucumbers packed jars that have 2 garlic cloves also included; let seal.

Sweet Pickles

2 C. vinegar
1 C. water
1½ T. mixed spices
1 T. grated horseradish
2 tsp. salt
2 T. alum

Wash cucumbers small or medium size and put into jars. Add vinegar, water, spices, horseradish, salt and alum. Seal with 2 piece lids, placing in cold packer filled wiht cold water. When water comes to a boil, turn off and let cool in water. When ready to use wash cucumbers, after draining off spice mixture. Cut into desired size; add 2½ C. white sugar and let stand at least 24 hours before using. Makes its own syrup. Enough for 2 quarts, if you need more liquid to fill jars, add extra vinegar to cover cucumbers.

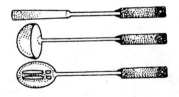

Cucumber Chips

14 dill size cucumbers
8 C. sugar
1 qt. vinegar

1 tsp. salt, not iodized
2 T. mixed pickling spices, tied in
a bag

Wash cucumbers well and pack in an enamel pan. Cover with boiling water. Pour this off each morning for 3 days and cover with fresh boiling water. On the fourth morning, slice the cucumbers into very thin slices and put back into the cleaned enamel pan. Combine sugar, vinegar, salt and mixed pickling spices. Boil hard. Pour hot syrup over sliced cucumbers. Each morning for three days pour off the syrup. Bring to boil and put back on the cucumbers. On the fourth day bring cucumbers and syrup to boil and put into hot sterilized jars. Wipe jar lips well and seal.

Hurry-Up Hamburger Mix

1½ lbs. ground beef
1 tsp. salt

1/8 tsp. pepper
1 can chicken gumbo soup

Set electric skillet at 350°. Cook and stir meat until crumbly and light brown. Add salt, pepper and soup; simmer at 190° for 15-20 minutes. Serve on buns with mustard, dill pickles and sliced onion.

Ice Box Pickles

4 C. sugar
½ C. salt
1½ tsp. celery seed
Cucumbers, thinly sliced

4 C. vinegar
1½ tsp. turmeric
1½ tsp. mustard seed
3 lg. onions, thinly sliced

Mix all ingredients except cucumbers and onions. Do not heat. Place cucumbers and onions in a covered container. Pour brine over them. Refrigerate. Wait at least 5 days before using.

Meat Sauce

1 onion
1 lb. hamburger
Red pepper
Sweet basil

1 clove garlic
1 (No. 2½) can tomatoes
1 can tomato paste

Chop onion and cook in olive oil. Add hamburger and cook until brown. Add rest of ingredients. Cook 2 hours.

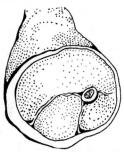

Casserole Sauce Mix

2 C. nonfat dry milk powder
¾ C. cornstarch
¼ C. powdered chicken bouillon
4 tsp. onion powder

1 tsp. dried thyme leaves
1 tsp. dried basil leaves
½ tsp. pepper

Use with chicken, tuna, macaroni and cheese. ¾ C. to a casserole.

Easy Strawberry Jam

1 qt. strawberries
1 T. butter

4 C. sugar
2 T. lemon juice

In Dutch oven size pan, combine strawberries and 2 C. sugar. Bring to boil over medium-high heat. Boil for 2 minutes. Add 2 C. more sugar and 1 T. butter. Bring back to boil and boil for 3 minutes. Mixture will boil to top of pan. Stir occasionally while cooking. Take off of heat and add lemon juice. Let stand, stirring occasionally until cold. Skim off white film on top.

Chicken Dressing

3 lbs. chicken
3 loaves bread
6 eggs
3 C. chicken broth
¾ T. pepper

1 t. celery salt
2 T. sage
4 tsp. salt
3 C. fresh ground onions
2 C. finely chopped celery

Simmer chicken with celery leaves until done. Remove chicken to cool; save broth. Remove skin and bones from chicken and put chicken through meat grinder. Cube bread slices. Dampen thoroughly with water and squeeze dry. Beat eggs; add chicken, then add bread and mix to a fine consistency. Add ground onions, chopped celery and the ground chicken. Mix again, then generously butter large roaster and pour in dressing. Preheat oven to 350°. Bake dressing 2½-3 hours or until firm. Baste occasionally with chicken broth. The recipe serves 25 people.

Zucchini Jam

5½ C. grated zucchini
6 C. sugar
1 C. water

2 T. lemon juice
1 (20 oz.) can crushed pineapple
2 (3 oz. ea.) pkgs. Jello, any flavor

Boil 6 minutes, zucchini, sugar and water. Add lemon juice and pineapple. Boil 6 minutes more. Add two 3 oz. each packages Jello. Boil 6 minutes more. Pour hot mixture into jars, put on lid and screw band. Jars will seal without processing if you put on lids immediately after you pour in hot mixture.

Beer Batter

1 egg
⅔ C. beer
¼ C. oil

2 tsp. sugar
2 tsp. salt
¾ C. flour

Blend ingredients together and dip fish in batter, fry in hot oil.

Sweet Pickles

8 qts. cucumbers
½ C. pickling salt
4 C. vinegar
8 C. sugar

1 tsp. turmeric
1 T. celery seed
1 T. mixed pickling spice

Wash cucumbers and place in a crock. Pour boiling water over them; let stand overnight. Drain and repeat for 6 days. On 7th day, drain; add salt. Cover with boiling water; let stand overnight. Drain. Prick cucumber or slice longer ones. Combine vinegar, 4 C. sugar, turmeric, celery seed and pickling spices. Heat and pour over cucumbers, each morning for two or more mornings. Pack pickles in jars. Add remaining sugar to mixture, heat to boiling and pour over pickles in the jar and seal.

Need A Gift?

For

- **Shower** • **Birthday** • **Mother's Day** •
  • **Anniversary** • **Christmas** •

Turn Page for Order Form
(Order Now While Supply Lasts!)

To Order Copies Of
Depression Times Cookbook

Please send me _____ copies of **Depression Times Cookbook** at $11.95 each plus $3.50 shipping. (Make checks payable to **Quixote Press.**)

Name _____

Street _____

City _____State _____Zip _____

Send Orders To:
Quixote Press
3544 Blakslee St.
Wever, IA 52658
1-800-571-2665

- -

To Order Copies Of
Depression Times Cookbook

Please send me _____ copies of **Depression Times Cookbook** at $11.95 each plus $3.50 shipping. (Make checks payable to **Quixote Press.**)

Name _____

Street _____

City _____State _____Zip _____

Send Orders To:
Quixote Press
3544 Blakslee St.
Wever, IA 52658
1-800-571-2665